GOOD AND EVIL

By Martin Buber

I AND THOU · Second Edition

Published by Charles Scribner's Sons

GOOD AND EVIL

Two Interpretations

I.
RIGHT AND WRONG

II.
IMAGES OF GOOD AND EVIL

by
MARTIN BUBER

Prentice Hall, Upper Saddle River, New Jersey 07458

©1997 by Prentice-Hall Inc.
Upper Saddle River, New Jersey 07458

Printed in the United States of America
30 29 28 27

ISBN 0-02-316280-5

Prentice-Hall International (UK) Limited, *London*
Prentice-Hall of Australia Pty. Limited, *Sydney*
Prentice-Hall Canada Inc., *Toronto*
Prentice-Hall Hispanoamericana, S.A., *Mexico*
Prentice-Hall of India Private Limited, *New Delhi*
Prentice-Hall of Japan, Inc., *Tokyo*
Pearson Education Asia Pte. Ltd., *Singapore*
Editoria Prentice-Hall do Brasil, Ltda., Rio De *Janeiro*

GOOD AND EVIL

Two Interpretations

FOREWORD

The two "interpretations" which are united in this
volume differ from one another in method and purpose, but they supplement each other to such an extent
that I have willingly accepted the suggestion to unite
them here in an external way as well.

Both are concerned with good and evil, but *Right
and Wrong* is concerned with its place in man's' ob-
servation of the human world, *Images* with its place
in the personal development of the individual man.
The first deals with the apparent contradiction which
holds sway in destiny, the second above all with the
factual conflict which holds sway in the soul. Here
an answer is sought to the question, "Why is evil so
powerful?", there to the question, "What is the origin
of evil?"

Thus one can describe *Images of Good and Evil* as
an interpretation because it proceeds from several Old

Israelitic and Old Persian myths. These myths portray in great images the twofold prehistorical origin of that which we call evil and thereby enable the modern thinker to point out what corresponds to this twofoldness in that biographical reality of present-day man which is known to us. *Right and Wrong* is interpretation in another sense. Here several Psalms are examined to discover how the gradually arising and growing insight into the relation between wrongdoing and true existence is expressed in them.

Taken together, the two books are to be regarded as a contribution to the foundation of an ontological ethics.

MARTIN BUBER

Jerusalem, December 31, 1952

CONTENTS

CONTENTS

IMAGES OF GOOD AND EVIL

Part Two

RIGHT AND WRONG

An Interpretation of Some Psalms

Translated by
RONALD GREGOR SMITH

PREFACE

In this book I discuss five psalms, all of which treat of the relation between right doing and wrong doing, between the rightdoers and the wrongdoers on earth, and so of the world struggle between good and evil.

These psalms, as can be seen from the many stylistic differences, undoubtedly are the work of different authors; but the men who speak in them are so near to one another in their basic view and attitude that one may see in their place a single figure, who is simply multiplied in them, namely, 'the Psalmist'. In fact, when these psalms are set in the right sequence they complete one another like the stages of a personal way—a way leading through moving and transforming experiences to one great insight.

This way begins (in Psalm 12) with the Psalmist confronted by a world dominated by the 'smooth tongue', by unscrupulous falsehood, and up to every

3

trick which makes the false appear and be accounted as the true, and violence as right order. Where is there a hiding-place for loyalty? The Psalmist is certain: God will now 'arise', take oppressed loyalty to Himself, and set up the reign of truth on earth.

Yet it seems to become still worse (Psalm 14): it seems as though everything were rotten, and no-one did right any more, no-one dared to do right; only a remnant, whom the psalmist feels to be 'his people', persists in righteousness. But the speaker does not even now lose his assurance of divine support. God, he knows, does not simply test, from above, the state of the human race, and prepare the downfall of evil: He gives the loyal remnant the favour of His presence.

But the psalmist's confidence is again and again deceived. No great turning-point appears and it is as though the 'shameless one' is right in his teaching that God does not trouble about the world of men. The speaker (Psalm 82) can only explain this increasingly strange situation by saying that God has given the rule over the earth to angels in order that they might do aright but that they, like the first men, are false to their orders. The Psalmist does not yet lose hope, however: in a vision his assurance is renewed. God will judge the bad judges and condemn them, like the first men, to mortality. And when the judgment is still not performed, he dares to call on God to 'arise' and carry it out.

But again he is disillusioned (Psalm 73). All around him the mean and vulgar flourish, while the righteous man suffers. And now it seems to him as though it could never be different upon earth. In vain he seeks another relation to God's omnipotence and man's destiny, one that might open out a prospect from this ambiguous existence into a future life filled with meaning. He is about to fall a prey to despair. Then unexpectedly, under the influence of an unprecedented illumination, there takes place in him a change which leads him on the way of God, towards His presence. With the change of heart there is a change of eye, and to his new view there is meaning in what for long was meaningless. Everything depends on the inner change; when this has taken place, and only then, the world changes.

The Psalmist recognises, and praises (Psalm 1), as the only irrefragable happiness, the happiness of the man who is walking in the way of God and drawing near to Him.

The interpretation of the five psalms which is given in this book is intended to make clear what they have to say to us about the difference between mere conscious being and true existence as the nearness of God. It may therefore be described as an essay in existential exegesis.

I. AGAINST THE GENERATION
OF THE LIE

Psalm 12

The lie is the specific evil which man has introduced into nature. All our deeds of violence and our misdeeds are only as it were a highly-bred development of what this and that creature of nature is able to achieve in its own way. But the lie is our very own invention, different in kind from every deceit that the animals can produce. A lie was possible only after a creature, man, was capable of conceiving the being of truth. It was possible only as directed against the conceived truth. In a lie the spirit practises treason against itself.

It has been asked why there is no prohibition of lying in the Decalogue. It is prohibited; but it appears only as a prohibition of the lying witness. For the Decalogue is concerned with the establishment and securing of the inner bonds of a community, and therefore every injustice is considered from its social aspect (in the widest sense), as injury done to the neighbour's sphere of life, and not in itself, as injury done to the structure of the spirit. But the more decisive the person's emergence in the course of historical development from the association of the community, and the more personal the individual's perception of himself and his fellow-men, the more is the suffering from the lie as such both felt and expressed.

This is a Psalm in which this feeling is at once heightened and differentiated. The speaker no longer suffers merely from liars, but from a generation of the lie, and the lie in this generation has reached the highest level of perfection as an ingeniously controlled means of supremacy. But the Psalmist is not content to utter his suffering and brand those who caused it; he also sees (for this Psalm is one of those prophetic Psalms which are built up round a vision) the beginning of the counter-action from above.

The key-words 'children of men', 'lip', 'smooth', 'tongue', 'speak', 'sayings', 'free/freedom', which recur twice or thrice in the Psalm, sketch the outlines of the subject. This subject is the negative influence exercised in this hour by a certain kind

of 'lips' ('smooth') and 'tongue' on human com-
munication by means of speech. More precisely,
the subject is the disintegration of human speech
as a result of this influence. The liberating act of
God and His 'sayings', the word of truth proceeding from Him, are opposed to this.

God is called upon to 'set free'. What He is to
free *from*, is the present state of affairs which is
characterised in what follows. The two basic qualities, on which men's common life rests, well-wish-
ing or the good will—that is, the readiness to fulfil
for the other what he may expect of me in our relation with one another—and loyalty or reliability—
that is, a responsible accord between my actions
and my explicit mind—have gone. They have disappeared so completely that the basis of men's
common life has been removed. The lie has taken
the place, as a form of life, of human truth, that is,
of the undivided seriousness of the human person
with himself and all his manifestations.

Of this element of the lie which now dominates
human intercourse three things are said, in relation
to its effect, to its structure, and its purpose. First,
those the Psalmist has in mind speak 'delusion'
—which of course does not mean they themselves
suffer from a vain delusion and express it, but with

9

their speech they breed 'delusion' in their hearers, they spin illusions for them; in particular they spin a way of thinking for them which they themselves do not follow. Instead of completing their fellow-man's experience and insight with the help of their own, as is required by men's common thinking and knowing, they introduce falsified material into his knowledge of the world and of life, and thus falsify the relations of his soul to being. Second, they speak with a double heart, literally 'with heart and heart'. This expression must be grasped in all its depth. The duplicity is not just between heart and mouth, but actually between heart and heart. In order that the lie may bear the stamp of truth, the liars as it were manufacture a special heart, an apparatus which functions with the greatest appearance of naturalness, from which lies well up to the 'smooth lips' like spontaneous utterances of experience and insight. Third, all this is the work of the mighty, in order to render tractable by their deceits those whom they have oppressed. Their tongues maintain them in their superiority. They 'speak great things' and by the speaking bind their bondslaves still more to them. And if they guess that rebellion is stirring in the minds of the oppressed and the hope awakening that 'the Lord is with us!', then they answer themselves 'Our lips are with us, who is lord over us?'.

That is the moment of vision, or rather of audition, for the Psalmist. He hears the presumption whispering in their secret hearts, and at the same moment he hears God speaking. God says that seeing the oppression of the poor, and hearing the sighing of the needy, He will 'now' arise. With this 'now' there breaks out in the midst of extreme trouble the manifestation of a salvation which is not just bound to come some time, but is always present and needs only to become effective. This 'now' is the decisive prophetic category. The 'day of the Lord', on which the enthroned One 'arises', and for terror and for rapture reveals his kingdom, which was the hidden meaning of creation from the beginning, is, in the power of the prophetic vision, this very present day. The Psalmists, who here as often prove themselves to be the heirs of this vision, know that the 'arising' means both judgement and 'the freeing of all the oppressed of the earth' (Ps. 76, 10). Our Psalm is specially emphatic that this judgement and this freeing are not two events, but one. 'I set him in freedom, at whom they puff', says God. He says of the oppressed man, at whom the smooth lips puff with their much speaking, that

11

He will set him in the freedom of God. He is not set in a different world; this world of ours, which is 'now' revealed as God's world, is from now on the world of salvation. No judgement beyond this is needed: it is not said, and does not need to be said, that the generation of the lie is set, or will be set, in perdition. Where they are is unveiled as nothing, and that is all. Those who walk about in wickedness in this hour of the world in which (as is said in the conclusion of the Psalm) 'vileness is exalted among the sons of men', have been revealed in their nothingness by the working of salvation; rather, their nothingness has become their reality, the only being they have is their nothingness.

The Psalmist has heard the sentence of God. He knows and bears witness that these words, like all God's words and like them alone, are 'pure,' that is, free of the dross of untruth which clings to every word of man. What the speaker says here of the words of God, with the most emphatic images he can command, goes beyond the occasion. The Psalmist is no longer thinking only of the word he has heard, but God's truth is opposed in a grand antithesis to the lie of the wicked. Once more, and more deeply than before, we feel that this generation is not opposed to God as speaking lies but as

12

being a lie. Thou—so the Psalmist addresses God
—Thou keepest Thy words, Thou keepest the truth;
so Thou wilt preserve from the generation of the
lie 'for the time of the world' 'him' of whom Thou
hast said Thou wouldst set him in freedom—that
is, each one of us poor and oppressed ones. For the
time of the world in our language we say 'for ever',
but the biblical language is far more correct, for
it is only the future history of the human race
which is involved here, and not eternity which is
over all history and over all time.

The question is forced upon us, how this 'for the
time of the world' is to be reconciled with the fact
that the Psalmist has apparently been talking of a
single generation, namely that contemporary with
himself. The answer can only be that also for future
periods of human history a reappearance of the
generation of the lie is again and again to be feared,
but that the word of God for ever guarantees his
existence to the man who is deceived and misused
by this ever-recurring generation. God will preserve
him, as each time of need comes, from the power
of the lie, by setting in freedom and salvation him
who is devoted to the truth. The truth is God's
alone, but there is a human truth, namely, to be
devoted to the truth. The lie is from time and will

be swallowed up by time; the truth, the divine truth, is from eternity and in eternity, and this devotion to the truth, which we call human truth, partakes of eternity.

II. THE RIFT

Psalm 14

O N A HASTY READING this Psalm seems (apart
from some doubtful passages) to be simple enough. The speaker—it is supposed—
is speaking of Israel and the nations. The nations
are 'shameless' and godless, their habits are 'corrupt' and 'abominable'; among them, as is repeatedly said, there is none that does good, none
understands any more what God desires of man,
none asks after God and His rule, they are all 'gone
aside' from their original humanity as willed in the
creation, they are altogether 'decaying,' like tainted
food. In contrast, the people of Israel, which is
'oppressed' and 'eaten up' by this society of evildoers, is apparently described as a 'proven generation,' whose refuge is God and whom God will free
from the others and restore to their former glory.
There have certainly been not a few among the
Jews who thought that this Psalm, understood in

15

this way, gives, in its crude generalisation, a picture of the historical human world and of the place which the Jewish people had and have in it, which, though unjust, nevertheless contains truth. In our time, especially, nothing is more understandable than this view, and nothing is more wrong-headed.

Nowhere in the Psalms or in any place in Scripture is such a general expression as the one used here, 'the shameless', intended of the heathen in distinction from the Jew. Nowhere do the words 'the children of men' indicate foreign nations in contrast to Israel. It is always *men* who are spoken of, simply men in the world, or men in the little land which is the home of the biblical speaker. In spite of everything there is a pitiable self-righteousness in understanding the great picture of God, looking down from heaven to earth and spying out a single man who enquires after Him, as meaning that the Lord is perfectly satisfied with all His Jews and therefore needs to have no review of them, whereas the nations only serve as the dark foil of such brilliant beams. Nor does it help to single out confession to God as the distinctive mark: every important biblical speaker is, like Jeremiah, put there as an 'assayer' to examine the extent to which pathetic confession of the lips enters the reality of

16

personal life; none of them could have preferred a Jew, full of talk about God and going against Him in his life, to one who was silent about God but followed Him.

But, it will at once be objected, the Psalmist expressly accuses the evildoers of 'eating up' his people; therefore they must be outside this people. That is so; but what he calls his people is only a part of the people which bears the name of Israel —that part, namely, which includes the righteous and oppressed. He no longer counts as part of his people the shameless, those gone aside, who oppress the righteous. Thus the prophetic conception, which is directed towards things to come, of the holy remnant which is the true people, is here concentrated in the consideration of the present. But the view of the others too, those who are "decayed', is prophetic: it is as a whole, that the same Isaiah who saw the holy remnant for what it was, saw the greater part of Israel which had fallen into corruption. It is true that for him they were 'this people', and the remnant was just the 'remnant', whereas for the Psalmist the proven generation is the real people. God's people, and the others are just the others; but they are so many that they seem to him to be 'all'. The falling away of the corrupt means Israel's falling asunder. What appears outwardly to be a unified nation is in truth torn in two—but of the two parts only one is still truly to be called Israel, a living organism; the other is nothing but decomposed tissue, the rotting substance of a people.

The Psalmist describes the Israel which is thus torn in two. There are the oppressors and there are the oppressed, the arrogant and the humble. Those say in their heart 'There is no God'. They do not say it aloud, it does not rise from the heart to the lips; with their lips they confess him. Even in their heart they do not mean, by what they say, to contest the existence of God. Why should there not be a God—so long as He does not bother Himself with what men are doing on earth! But the truth is that God watches what His creatures are making of themselves. He sees how men 'eat up' men; and (this is the readiest explanation of the difficult text of verse 4) this is not a food—like the animal sacrifice which is called the 'bread of God'—over which one may call upon the name of God. The Psalmist gazes in prophetic vision upon what is to come: those who have fallen away rush again on their prey, but suddenly they are filled with terror: there, in the midst of those who they thought were abandoned to an arbitrary fate, the Presence of God appears, even that God who they thought was far from men and their doings, but who is in truth the refuge of the oppressed. And His word thunders upon them.

At this point the prophetic Psalmist unites his Messianic prayer and his Messianic promise. Israel's liberation and salvation can only come 'out of Zion', and it does not make sense to understand this 'out of Zion' topographically. The Zion of righteousness fulfilled in the land of Israel is what must be meant. For the 'remnant', which has now truly become the people of God, the great turning-point draws near.

A late interpreter of the Psalms like myself cannot be satisfied, as the Psalmist was, with a simple division of Israel, just as I could not be satisfied with such a division of the human world. We see the rift between those who do violence and those to whom violence is done, the rift between those who are true to God and the apostate element, running not merely through every nation, but also through every group in a nation, and even through every soul. Only in times of great crisis does the hidden rift in a people become apparent.

III. JUDGEMENT ON THE JUDGES

Psalm 82

THE DEEPER my experience of life, the more thoroughly do I understand this Psalm, which is so variously interpreted and yet in the end is so simple. It must, indeed, more than any other Psalm be considered by itself.

First we must survey its structure, which is sublimely severe and consistent.

The structure is determined by the fact that the Psalm, unlike most, does not express an emotion but presents a visionary event. In the midst of this event are two speeches of God, uttered at two different stages of the event. These speeches are enclosed within three sayings of the Psalmist. The first saying tells us about the circumstances of the event, the second leads from the first to the second stage of the event, while the third, with which the Psalmist concludes, leaves the event which has been contemplated, and, as it were inferring from it, calls directly upon the God Who has been at work on it.

The message of the Psalm is once again made clear by the recurring key-words. There are five such words, two of them primary, recurring four or five times, and three secondary, recurring only twice. The primary words are 'God, gods', and 'judge, do justice, judgement'. God here stands in judgement upon gods, in respect of their judging. The secondary key-words are 'earth', 'weak', and 'wicked'. The Psalmist's concern is not with heaven but with the earth, the earth of man, and within this human world with the weak, the afflicted, the wretched and needy (the synonyms serve to strengthen the essential point)—and the concern is that these receive justice in face of the wicked. God judges the 'gods', because in their function as judges they do not let the weak of the earth receive justice.

The picture of the situation with which the Psalmist opens is that God presides over a 'congregation', more precisely, a community of beings gathered together either by appointment or by a summons (in this case by a summons). So Samuel presides over the band of prophets, of which he is the head, as leader of the choir (I Sam. 19, 20)—

except that his upright position, in contrast to the cowering of those round about him (as we can still see today among the dervishes), is emphasised, whereas in the picture of the Psalm God clearly towers over those who stand in a circle around Him. And further, God's presiding signifies a judgement. The gathering has been summoned by God in order that He may pass judgement on those who are assembled. Who then are these? Their company is first described as an 'El'-company, that is, as a company of beings endowed with power of divine origin, a company of beings whose power has been lent to them by God, the only giver of power. This is how the Bible speaks of powerful mountains or of the fixed stars, in order to point to the divine *dunamis* from which their majesty springs.

But then those beings are themselves called 'gods'. It is sufficiently clear from the second speech of God, which pronounces the judgement on the 'gods' that they must die 'like men', that this description of them as gods is not to be understood as a metaphor for human authority. In order to grasp the nature and range of influence of those beings, we must look at some of the turning-points in the relation of Biblical religion to the history of the nations.

Even the earliest writing prophets were faced with the fact that other nations possessed similar traditions of their wandering and their settlement to those of Israel, and that each of these nations worshipped its tribal god as the leader of those marches by means of which the tribe or association of tribes had grown to be a nation and had entered the history of the nations. The question which faced the prophets was, how are these traditions to be reconciled with the basic factor of Israel's *election*, which presupposes the sovereignty of YHWH over the nations from which He had made His choice? We find the prophets' answer in the words of Amos (9, 7) that it was He who had led the other nations, as He had led Israel, in their history-making wandering and settling, whereas to Israel alone did God condescend to give His immediate company (Amos 3, 2). This means that all the gods of the nations were characterised as being masks or caricatures of the one true Liberator of the nations, the God of history to whom Israel pays homage. But now this exclusive faith is opposed by the experience of history that even in times when Israel was loyal to its covenantal relation with God, one of those neighbouring nations which had been led to that place by YHWH Himself, from time to time defeated Israel in battle—an experience which, especially in its most sensitive form under Josiah, excited very serious doubts and produced many different answers. One of these answers was that the national gods were allowed a kind of independent existence and with it independence of historical action, so that the defeats of an Israel true to its Covenant could be ascribed to them. Their historical power was, however, continually limited by the power of YHWH, which was paramount over them all and in the last resort was alone decisive. A notable witness to this view is the text of Jephthah's message to the King of the Ammonites— which presumably originates in the time of Josiah. First Jephthah proposes that the frontiers of each territory, which were laid down for each people by its God, should be respected by the other people, and here YHWH is seen as being on the same plane as the other national gods. If this, however, is not granted, then, so the message continues, 'May YHWH the Judge judge today between the sons of Israel and the sons of Ammon'. Here Israel's God is no longer one among the gods of the nations, but the Sovereign over the world of the nations, Who possesses the inalienable right of decision as to which of them is right and which is wrong, and

Who gives judgement in accordance with His decision: that is, He determines the history of the nations, He is the Judge. In the course of the message we move from the realm of relative historical powers into that of the absolute historical power.

From this point a way leads to the historical perspective of the Book of Daniel, where each land and nation is represented by an angel prince, and Israel too, like Persia and Greece, possesses its angel and so no longer has its direct relation to the Lord of the nations. The most important stage on this way is our Psalm.

In order to pass judgement on the heavenly princes of the nations God the Judge has entered their assembly, which He has summoned. This is not the cosmic circle of a heavenly host, such as surrounds the supreme throne in the prophet's vision (I Kings 22, 19), and from which cosmic powers are commissioned to lead human rulers astray in foolish historical actions. The assembled powers are not cosmic in nature, but historical, as we know them from the Book of Daniel. That is clear from the first speech of God. The chief function with which they are entrusted is that of judging the earth and they have clearly not to judge alongside one another, but the earth is divided

among them; to each a land and a nation is specially
allotted. Each of them is a governor for God, and
each, like the 'judges' of the early period of Israel,
is clearly called to dispense justice to his people,
both outwardly and inwardly. Outwardly they may
all have fulfilled their office honourably, and each
of them may have adequately represented the cause
of his nation in so far as that cause was righteous;
for God does not speak of this. It is unjust rule of
which He accuses them all, more precisely, failure
to act against social injustice. Instead of fulfilling
their task of helping the powerless and the unpro-
tected to obtain justice in face of the oppresser,
they have adjudged to this man, just because he
had the power, all that he coveted.

What sounds forth here from the mouth of God
is, translated into myth, the demand made by the
prophets upon the kings of Israel and their accusation of these kings. From the very beginning of
the time of the State the prophets regarded their
anointing of the kings as the sacramental seal upon
the commission of the kings to build up, as God's
representatives, a kingdom of righteousness. The
Psalmists give a personal expression to this content.
They address the king (45, 7): 'Thou hast loved
righteousness, and hated wickedness: therefore

God, thy God, hath anointed thee . . .' They be-
seech God (72, 1f.) to give the king His judgements, that he may rule the people with righteousness. His saving righteousness towards the 'needy'
is here depicted in the same speech in which God's
righteousness in other ways is described: the function of God's representative has as its inner meaning an imitation of the Lord of the world. God's
earthly representative must manifest God's righteousness. If he fails to do so he has become un-
worthy of his office and is 'rejected', even if he has
rendered justice to his people outwardly—for the
prophetic insight teaches that a human community
can only truly exist in so far as it becomes a true
community of human beings.

As God has set the king over Israel, so in our
Psalm he has set the intermediary beings—here
called 'gods' and elsewhere called 'sons of God', over
the nations of the earth, each over one of the nations, in order to manifest in its structure and gov-
ernment the justice of the Judge of the world. In
his first speech God accuses them of having judged
not in accordance with his order and regulation,
but in the manner of what is false and evil: for
they have confirmed and substantiated in their
power those who have acted wickedly against God's

justice, instead of depriving evil of its power by means of the supreme authority which has been given to them. But a secret respite is still granted to them; after the accusation comes the warning. Once more they are told what their office is: their judgements must be for the weak, it is their duty to make the good cause of the oppressed prevail in the world, they are to save the persecuted from the high-handed persecutors.

But now a terrible thing comes to pass: the governors do not obey the warning of the Ruler either. We learn of this passive rebellion of the angels in the form of an intermediate speech of the Psalmist. He does not say, however, that they refuse to obey. He says rather that they do not know and cannot distinguish. They do not understand the essence and the intention of God's word. To translate into modern forms of speech, they wish to conduct the history of the human race as a continuation of the history of nature and they persist in the delusion that the way of man can be determined from the general customs of the animals. It is this delusion which makes possible the self-glorification in which they indulge. It is only as biological powers that they can regard themselves as sovereigns in the world of men: as soon as they acknowledge the authority of a divine justice they are not more than ruling subjects. In the 'darkness' of this delusion the intermediary beings walk to and fro beneath the word of the Judge and disregard it.

Then God pronounces sentence upon them, and in such a way that 'all the foundations of the earth stagger'. For with God there is no division between sentence and execution. The sentence is that they are no longer gods. Once, says God to those rebellious ones, I made you to be gods, sons of God, and to live with me in my eternity; but now, since you have like human princes failed to keep the command of my righteousness, I sentence you to human death.

This is the end of God's speech and the end—with only a hint of the fall of the 'gods'—of the visionary event of which the Psalmist has to inform us. But his song is not ended. Rather now, for the first time, the real Psalm is heard, in only a few words, and yet saying all that has still to be said. The speaker turns away from us to God. 'In my vision', he says to him, 'I have seen how Thou dost bring to destruction the rule over history of Thy rebellious governors. So be it, Lord. Since those who were entrusted with the office of judge succumbed to injustice, do Thou abolish the inter-

mediary rule, renounce the useless work of under-
lings and Thyself judge the world immediately in
Thy justice. Thine are the nations, lead them as
thine own! Close the history of man which is a prey
to delusion and wickedness, open his true history!'

A Jew of our time, Franz Kafka, has in his writings provided a commentary to the presuppositions
of this Psalm. I say, to its presuppositions, not to
the Psalm itself. Kafka describes the human world
as one which is given over to the intermediary
beings, with which they play their confused game.
From the unknown One who gave this world into
their impure hands, no message of comfort or
promise penetrates to us. He is, but he is not
present.

What has not entered into the view of Kafka, of
the man of our time, is to be found in this Psalm.

IV. THE HEART DETERMINES

Psalm 73

WHAT IS REMARKABLE about this poem—composed of descriptions, of a story and of confessions—is that a man tells how he reached the true meaning of his experience of life, and that this meaning borders directly on the eternal.

For the most part we understand only gradually the decisive experiences which we have in our relation with the world. First we accept what they seem to offer us, we express it, we weave it into a 'view', and then think we are aware of our world. But we come to see that what we look on in this view is only an appearance. Not that our experiences have deceived us. But we had turned them to our use, without penetrating to their heart. What is it that teaches us to penetrate to their heart? Deeper experience.

The man who speaks in this Psalm tells us how

31

he penetrated to the heart of a weighty group of experiences—those experiences which show that the wicked prosper.

Apparently, then, the question is not what was the real question for Job—why the good do not prosper—but rather its obverse, as we find it most precisely, and probably for the first time, expressed in Jeremiah (12, 1): 'Why does the way of the wicked prosper?'

Nevertheless, the Psalm begins with a prefatory sentence in which, rightly considered, Job's question may be found hidden.

This sentence, the foreword to the Psalm, is

> Surely God is good to Israel:
> To the pure in heart.

It is true that the Psalmist is here concerned not with the happiness or unhappiness of the person, but with the happiness or unhappiness of Israel. But the experience behind the speeches of Job, as is evident in many of them, is itself not merely personal, but is the experience of Israel's suffering both in the catastrophe which led to the Babylonian exile and in the beginning of the exile itself. Certainly only one who had plumbed the depths of personal suffering could speak in this way. But the speaker is a man of Israel in Israel's bitter hour of need, and in his personal suffering the suffering of Israel has been concentrated, so that what he now has to suffer he suffers as Israel. In the destiny of an authentic person the destiny of his people is gathered up, and only now becomes truly manifest.

Thus the Psalmist, whose theme is the fate of the person, also begins with the fate of Israel. Behind his opening sentence lies the question 'Why do things go badly with Israel?' And first he answers, 'Surely, God is good to Israel', and then he adds, by way of explanation, 'to the pure in heart'. On first glance this seems to mean that it is only to the impure in Israel that God is not good, He is good to the pure in Israel, they are the 'holy remnant', the true Israel, to whom He is good. But that would lead to the assertion that things go well with this remnant, and the questioner had taken as his starting-point the experience that things went ill with Israel, not excepting indeed this part of it. The answer, understood in this way, would be no answer.

We must go deeper in this sentence. The questioner had drawn from the fact that things go ill with Israel the conclusion that therefore God is not good to Israel. But only one who is not pure in heart draws such a conclusion. One who is pure in heart, one who becomes pure in heart, cannot draw any such conclusion. For he experiences that God is good to him. But this does not mean that God rewards him with his goodness. It means, rather, that God's goodness is revealed to him who is pure in heart: he experiences this goodness. In so far as Israel is pure in heart, becomes pure in heart, it experiences God's goodness.

Thus the essential dividing line is not between men who sin and men who do not sin, but between those who are pure in heart and those who are impure in heart. Even the sinner, whose heart becomes pure, experiences God's goodness as it is revealed to him. As Israel purifies its heart, it experiences that God is good to it.

It is from this standpoint that everything that is said in the Psalm about 'the wicked' is to be understood. The 'wicked' are those who deliberately persist in impurity of heart.

The state of the heart determines whether a man lives in the truth, in which God's goodness is experienced, or in the semblance of truth, where the fact that it 'goes ill' with him is confused with the illusion that God is not good to him.

The state of the heart determines. That is why 'heart' is the dominant key-word in this Psalm, which recurs six times.

And now, after this basic theme has been stated, the speaker begins to tell of the false ways in his experience of life.

Seeing the prosperity of 'the wicked' daily and hearing their braggart speech has brought him very near to the abyss of despairing unbelief, of the inability to believe any more in a living God active in life. 'But I, a little more and my feet had turned aside, a mere nothing and my steps had stumbled.' He goes so far as to be jealous of 'the wicked' for their privileged position.

It is not envy which he feels, it is jealousy, that it is *they* who are manifestly preferred by God. That it is indeed they, is proved to him by their being sheltered from destiny. For them there are not,[1] as for all the others, those constraining and confining 'bands' of destiny; 'they are never in the trouble of man'. And so they deem themselves superior to all, and stalk around with their 'sound and fat bellies', and when one looks in their eyes, which protrude from the fatness of their faces, one

[1]In what follows I read, as is almost universally accepted, *lamo tam* instead of *lemotam*.

sees 'the paintings of the heart', the wish-images of their pride and their cruelty, flitting across. Their relation to the world of their fellow-men is arrogance and cunning, craftiness and exploitation. 'They speak oppression from above' and 'set their mouth to the heavens'. From what is uttered by this mouth set to the heavens, the Psalmist quotes two characteristic sayings which were supposed to be familiar. In the one (introduced by 'therefore', meaning 'therefore they say') they make merry over God's relation to 'his people'. Those who speak are apparently in Palestine as owners of great farms, and scoff at the prospective return of the landless people from exile, in accordance with the prophecies: the prophet of the Exile has promised them water (Isa. 41, 17f.), and 'they may drink their fill of water', they will certainly not find much more here unless they become subject to the speakers. In the second saying they are apparently replying to the reproaches levelled against them: they were warned that God sees and knows the wrongs they have done, but the God of heaven has other things to do than to concern Himself with such earthly matters: 'How does God know? Is there knowledge in the Most High?' And God's attitude confirms

36

them, those men living in comfortable security:
'they have reached power', theirs is the power.

That was the first section of the Psalm, in which
the speaker depicted his grievous experience, the
prosperity of the wicked. But now he goes on to
explain how his understanding of this experience
has undergone a fundamental change.

Since he had again and again to endure, side by
side, his own suffering and their 'grinning' well-
being, he is overcome: 'it is not fitting that I should
make such comparisons, as my own heart is not
pure.' And he proceeded to purify it. In vain. Even
when he succeeded in being able 'to wash his hands
in innocence' (which does not mean an action or
feeling of self-righteousness, but the genuine, second and higher purity which is won by a great
struggle of the soul), the torment continued, and
now it was like a leprosy to him; and as leprosy
is understood in the Bible as a punishment for the
disturbed relation between heaven and earth, so
each morning, after each pain-torn night, it came
over the Psalmist—'It is a chastisement—why am I
chastised?' And once again there arose the contrast
between the horrible enigma of the happiness of
the wicked and his suffering.

At this point he was tempted to accuse God as Job did. He felt himself urged to 'tell how it is'. But he fought and conquered the temptation. The story of this conquest follows in the most vigorous form which the speaker has at his disposal, as an appeal to God. He interrupts his objectivised account and addresses God. If I had followed my inner impulse, he says to Him, 'I should have betrayed the generation of thy sons'. The generation of the sons of God! Then he did not know that the pure in heart are the children of God, now he does know. He would have betrayed them if he had arisen and accused God. For they continue in suffering and do not complain. The words sound to us as though the speaker contrasted these 'children of God' with Job, the complaining 'servant of God'.

He, the Psalmist, was silent even in the hours when the conflict of the human world burned into his purified heart. But now he summoned every energy of thought in order to 'know' the meaning of this conflict. He strained the eyes of the spirit in order to penetrate the darkness which hid the meaning from him. But he always perceived only the same conflict ever anew, and this perception itself seemed to him now to be a part of that 'trouble' which lies on all save those 'wicked' men

—even on the pure in heart. He had become one of these, yet he still did not recognise that 'God is good to Israel'.

'Until I came into the sanctuaries of God.' Here the real turning-point in this exemplary life is reached.

The man who is pure in heart, I said, experiences that God is good to him. He does not experience it as a consequence of the purification of his heart, but because only as one who is pure in heart is he able to come to the sanctuaries. This does not mean the Temple precincts in Jerusalem, but the sphere of God's holiness, the holy mysteries of God. Only to him who draws near to these is the true meaning of the conflict revealed.

But the true meaning of the conflict, which the Psalmist expresses here only for the other side, the 'wicked', as he expressed it in the opening words for the right side, for the 'pure in heart', is not—as the reader of the following words is only too easily misled into thinking—that the present state of affairs is replaced by a future state of affairs of a quite different kind, in which 'in the end' things go well with the good and badly with the bad; in the language of modern thought the meaning is that the bad do not truly exist, and their 'end' brings about only this change, that they now inescapably experience their non-existence, the suspicion of which they had again and again succeeded in dispelling. Their life was 'set in slippery places'; it was so arranged as to slide into the knowledge of their own nothingness; and when this finally happens, 'in a moment', the great terror falls upon them and they are consumed with terror. Their life has been a shadow structure in a dream of God's. God awakes, shakes off the dream, and disdainfully watches the dissolving shadow image.

This insight of the Psalmist, which he obtained as he drew near to the holy mysteries of God, where the conflict is resolved, is not expressed in the context of his story, but in an address to 'his Lord'. And in the same address he confesses, with harsh self-criticism, that at the same time the state of error in which he had lived till then and from which he had suffered so much was revealed to him: 'When my heart rose up in me, and I was pricked in my reins, brutish was I and ignorant, I have been as a beast before Thee.'

With this 'before Thee' the middle section of the Psalm significantly concludes, and at the end of the first line of the last section (after the description and the story comes the confession) the words

are significantly taken up The words 'And I am'
at the beginning of the verse are to be understood
emphatically: 'Nevertheless I am', 'Nevertheless I
am continually with Thee'. God does not count it
against the heart which has become pure that it
was earlier accustomed 'to rise up'. Certainly even
the erring and struggling man was 'with Him', for
the man who struggles for God is near Him even
when he imagines that he is driven far from God.
That is the reality which we learn from the revelation to Job out of the storm, in the hour of Job's
utter despair (30, 20-22) and utter readiness (31, 35-
39). But what the Psalmist wishes to teach us, in
contrast to the Book of Job, is that the fact of his
being with God is revealed to the struggling man
in the hour when—not led astray by doubt and
despair into treason, and become pure in heart—
'he comes to the sanctuaries of God'. Here he receives the revelation of the 'continually'. He who
draws near with a pure heart to the divine mystery,
learns that he is continually with God.

It is a revelation. It would be a misunderstand-
ing of the whole situation to look on this as a pious
feeling. From man's side there is no continuity,
only from God's side. The Psalmist has learned that
God and he are continually with one another. But

41

he cannot express his experience as a word of God. The teller of the primitive stories made God say to the fathers and to the first leaders of the people: 'I am with thee', and the word 'continually' was unmistakably heard as well. Thereafter, this was no longer reported and we hear it again only in rare prophecies. A Psalmist (23, 5) is still able to say to God: 'Thou art with me.' But when Job (29, 5) speaks of God's having been with him in his youth, the fundamental word, the 'continually', has disappeared. The speaker in our Psalm is the first and only one to insert it expressly. He no longer says: 'Thou art with me', but 'I am continually with thee'. It is not, however, from his own consciousness and feeling that he can say this, for no man is able to be continually turned to the presence of God: he can say it only in the strength of the revelation that God is continually with him.

The Psalmist no longer dares to express the central experience as a word of God; but he expresses it by a gesture of God. God has taken his right hand —as a father, so we may add, in harmony with that expression 'the generation of thy children', takes his little son by the hand in order to lead him. More precisely, as in the dark a father takes his little son by the hand, certainly in order to lead him, but primarily in order to make present to him, in the warm touch of coursing blood, the fact that he, the father, is continually with him.

It is true that immediately after this the leading itself is expressed: 'Thou dost guide me with thy counsel.' But ought this to be understood as meaning that the speaker expects God to recommend to him in the changing situations of his life what he should do and what he should refrain from doing? That would mean that the Psalmist believes that he now possesses a constant oracle, who would exonerate him from the duty of weighing up and deciding what he must do. Just because I take this man so seriously I cannot understand the matter in this way. The guiding counsel of God seems to me to be simply the divine Presence communicating itself direct to the pure in heart. He who is aware of this Presence acts in the changing situations of his life differently from him who does not perceive this Presence. The Presence acts as counsel: God counsels by making known that He is present. He has led his son out of darkness into the light, and now he can walk in the light. He is not relieved of taking and directing his own steps.

The revealing insight has changed life itself, as well as the meaning of the experience of life. It also changes the perspective of death. For the 'oppressed' man death was only the mouth towards which the sluggish stream of suffering and trouble flows. But now it has become the event in which God—the continually Present One, the One who grasps the man's hand, the Good One—'takes' a man.

The tellers of the legends had described the translation of the living Enoch and the living Elijah to heaven as 'a being taken', a being taken away by God Himself. The Psalmists transferred the description from the realm of miracle to that of personal piety and its most personal expression. In a Psalm which is related to our Psalm not only in language and style but also in content and feeling, the forty-ninth, there are these words: 'But God will redeem my soul from the power of Sheol, when He takes me.' There is nothing left here of the mythical idea of a translation. But not only that— there is nothing left of heaven either. There is nothing here about being able to go after death into heaven. And, so far as I see, there is nowhere in the 'Old Testament' anything about this.

It is true that the sentence in our Psalm which follows the words, 'Thou shalt guide me with thy counsel', seems to contradict this. It once seemed to me to be indeed so, when I translated it as 'And afterwards thou dost take me up to glory'. But I can no longer maintain this interpretation. In the original text there are three words. The first, 'afterwards', is unambiguous—'After thou hast guided me with thy counsel through the remainder of my life', that is, 'at the end of my life'. The second word needs more careful examination. For us who have grown up in the conceptual world of a later doctrine of immortality it is almost self-evident that we should understand 'Thou shalt take me' as 'Thou shalt take me up'. The hearer or reader of that time understood simply, 'Thou shalt take me away'. But does the third word, *kabod*, not contradict this interpretation? Does it not say *whither* I shall be taken, namely to 'honour' or 'glory'? No, it does not say this. We are led astray into this reading by understanding 'taking up' instead of 'taking'.

This is not the only passage in the scriptures where death and *kabod* meet. In the song of Isaiah on the dead king of Babylon, who once wanted to ascend into heaven like the day star, there are these words (14, 18): 'All the kings of the nations, all of them, lie in *kabod*, in glory, every one in his own house, but thou wert cast forth away from thy sepulchre.' He is refused an honourable grave because he has destroyed his land and slain his people. *Kabod* in death is granted to the others, because they have uprightly fulfilled the task of their life. *Kabod*, whose root meaning is the radiation of the inner 'weight' of a person, belongs to the earthly side of death. When I have lived my life, says our Psalmist to God, I shall die in *kabod*, in the fulfilment of my existence. In my death the coils of Sheol will not embrace me, but thy hand will grasp me. 'For', as is said in another Psalm related in kind to this one, the sixteenth, 'Thou wilt not leave my soul to Sheol'.

Sheol, the realm of nothingness, in which, as a later text explains (Eccl. 9.10), there is neither activity nor consciousness, is not contrasted with a kingdom of heavenly bliss. But over against the realm of nothing there is God. The 'wicked' have in the end a direct experience of their non-being, the 'pure in heart' have in the end a direct experience of the Being of God.

This sense of *being taken* is now expressed by the Psalmist in the unsurpassably clear cry, 'Whom have I in heaven!' He does not aspire to enter heaven after death, for God's home is not in heaven, so that heaven is empty. But he knows that in death he will cherish no desire to remain on earth, for now he will soon be wholly 'with Thee'—here the word recurs for the third time—with Him who 'has taken' him. But he does not mean by this what we are accustomed to call personal immortality, that is, continuation in the dimension of time so familiar to us in this our mortal life. He knows that after death 'being with Him' will no longer mean, as it does in this life, 'being separated from Him'. The Psalmist now says with the strictest clarity what must now be said: it is not merely his flesh which vanishes in death, but also his heart, that inmost personal organ of the soul, which formerly 'rose up' in rebellion against the human fate and which he then 'purified' till he became pure in heart—this personal soul also vanishes. But He who was the true part and true fate of this person, the 'rock' of this heart, God, is eternal. It is into His eternity that he who is pure in heart moves in death, and this eternity is something absolutely different from any kind of time.

Once again the Psalmist looks back at the 'wicked', the thought of whom had once so stirred him. Now he does not call them the wicked, but 'they that are far from Thee'.

In the simplest manner he expresses what he has learned: since they are far from God, from Being, they are lost. And once more the positive follows the negative, once more, for the third and last time, that 'and I', 'and for me', which here means "nevertheless for me'. 'Nevertheless for me the good is to draw near to God.' Here, in this conception of the good, the circle is closed. To him who may draw near to God, the good is given. To an Israel which is pure in heart the good is given, because it may draw near to God. Surely, God is good to Israel.

The speaker here ends his confession. But he does not yet break off. He gathers everything together. He has made his refuge, his 'safety', 'in his Lord'—he is sheltered in Him. And now, still turned to God, he speaks his last word about the task which is joined to all this, and which he has set himself, which God has set him—'To tell of all Thy works'. Formerly he was provoked to tell of the *appearance*, and he resisted. Now he knows, he has the *reality* to tell of: the works of God. The first of his telling, the tale of the work which God has performed with him, in this Psalm.

In this Psalm two kinds of men seem to be contrasted with one another, the 'pure in heart' and 'the wicked'. But that is not so. The 'wicked', it is true, are clearly one kind of men, but the others are not. A man is as a 'beast' and purifies his heart, and behold, God holds him by the hand. That is not a kind of men. Purity of heart is a state of being. A man is not pure in kind, but he is able to be or become pure, rather he is only essentially pure when he has become pure, and even then he does not thereby belong to a kind of men. The 'wicked', that is, the bad, are not contrasted with good men. The good, says the Psalmist, is 'to draw near to God'. He does not say that those near to God are good. But he does call the bad 'those who are far from God'. In the language of modern thought that means that there are men who have no share in existence, but there are no men who possess existence. Existence cannot be possessed, but only shared in. One does not rest in the lap of existence, but one draws near to it. 'Nearness' is nothing but such a drawing and coming near continually and as long as the human person lives.

The dynamic of fairness and nearness is broken by death when it breaks the life of the person. With death there vanishes the heart, that inwardness of man, out of which arise the 'pictures' of the imagination, and which rises up in defiance, but which can also be purified.

Separate souls vanish, separation vanishes. Time

which has been lived by the soul vanishes with the soul, we know of no duration in time. Only the 'rock' in which the heart is concealed, only the rock of human hearts does not vanish. For it does not stand in time. The time of the world disappears before eternity, but existing man dies into eternity as into the perfect existence.

V. THE WAYS

Psalm 1

Often, when I open the Psalms, I begin by looking at the first, which was early understood as a proem to the Psalter. I am inclined to think that even the oldest collection of Psalms (perhaps brought together under Hezekiah) was introduced by this Psalm. The intention behind that collection may have been to complete the 'Torah' or 'direction' (which means a book of teachings and laws edited at that time and ascribed to Moses) by means of hymns and songs of a 'directing' kind. Here 'to direct' means to show the way which man should 'choose' (Ps. 25, 12), and that means to teach the man to distinguish this way, the right way, from the other, wrong ways. The right way, the way of God, is followed by 'the proven ones'. Those who continue on their own way, and refuse to go that way, are called 'the wicked', those who miss that way again and again are called sinners. The real struggle of the direction is therefore with the wicked, whereas the 'good' and 'upright' God again and again 'directs sinners in the way' (Ps. 25, 8), that is, helps them to find the way back.

By these simple presuppositions of the 'directing' hymns and songs we may explain the key-words of this Psalm. These words are 'way', 'direction', 'the proven ones', 'the wicked', 'sinners'. At the same time it becomes clear why the word 'wicked' occurs as frequently as 'proven' and 'sinners' together. The recurrence of the key-words is a basic law of composition in the Psalms. This law has a poetic significance—rhythmical correspondence of sound values—as well as a hermeneutical one: the Psalm provides its own interpretation, by repetition of what is essential to its understanding. This is why it often refuses, as here, to vary the expression of a certain subject, and is not afraid to repeat, as in the last part of this Psalm, the same leading description in three successive sentences. It is important to recognise (the Psalm emphasizes by this device) what the wicked are in relation to the way and the direction, to the proven ones and the sinners.

But when I open the Psalms what moves me to

look at this one is something else—the word with which it begins, and therefore the word with which the whole Psalter begins. It may be translated by 'O happiness!'. In this Psalm it is 'O the happiness of of the man . . .'. This is not a wish and not a promise. It is not that the man deserves happiness or that he may be certain of being happy whether in this earthly life or in another, future life. It is a joyful cry and a passionate statement—'how happy this man is!'

The theme of this Psalm is happiness, more precisely, true happiness, the truly happy man. This addition, 'true', 'truly', is indeed not explicit, as it might be in a philosophical study of the virtuous man which speaks of his having 'true' happiness. But of course the Psalmist, too, wants to indicate a happiness which is not obvious to all eyes, which is perhaps not even properly credible, since common experience knows nothing of it, though knowing something of the unhappiness of the man described in the Psalm. The Psalmist obviously also wants to say, 'Lo, there is a secret happiness hidden by the hands of life itself, which balances and outbalances all unhappiness. You do not see it, but it is true happiness, the only true happiness.' That is why he can dare to explain, in face of everyday appearances, which show the abundant failures of the good, that everything done by this man succeeds. Perhaps the Psalmist even intends to hearten the very man of whom he speaks against the despairing moods of a Job, by helping him to distinguish between apparent and true happiness, and by teaching him to penetrate into the profundities of true happiness and to feel it more passionately. And yet the Psalmist has obviously another purpose than the philosopher, who tells us that virtue is its own reward. It is true that the two sayings have something in common. But what they have in common is not the thing that matters, and if the philosopher's saying were to be brought to the Psalmist's notice and explained to him he would be speechless and could only shake his head. For what he really means is completely untouched by what the philosopher could say to him about the 'self-enjoyment' of the moral man. What he means about the life of the man of whom he speaks cannot be grasped by means of moral values; and what he means about his happiness has its home in another sphere from that of a man's self-satisfaction. Both the conduct of the man's life and his happiness in their nature transcend the realm of ethics as well as that of self-consciousness. Both are to be under-

54

stood only from a man's intercourse with God, which is the basic theme of the Book of Psalms.

This becomes most clear at the end of the poem where with concluding precision the way of the proven ones and the way of the wicked are contrasted. Of the way of the wicked it is said that it 'peters out'. That means that the men who go this way learn somewhere or other, at some point in their journey, that what they all the time had taken to be a way is no way, that this alleged way leads nowhere. And now they can see neither before nor after, their life now is wayless. If something of this kind were said to someone who had not read our Psalm, he would expect to hear now the opposite about 'the way' of the proven ones —that its character as a way becomes increasingly clear, till finally the goal which had hitherto been only glimpsed flashes with power upon the eyes of the man on the way. But this is not what the Psalmist says at this decisive point. He says rather that God 'knows' the way of the righteous. Taken according to normal linguistic usage, this sentence is not really intelligible. How should the fact that Gods knows this way correspond to the fact that the way of the wicked peters out? The commentators who cling to the normal usage make vain efforts to get rid of the difficulty. We can reach a clear understanding of the point only if we realise that the original meaning of the Hebrew verb 'to recognise, to know', in distinction from Western languages, belongs not to the sphere of reflection but to that of contact. The decisive event for 'knowing' in biblical Hebrew is not that one looks at an object, but that one comes into touch with it. This basic difference is developed in the realm of a relation of the soul to other beings, where the fact of mutuality changes everything. At the centre is not a perceiving of one another, but the contact of being, intercourse. This theme of 'knowing' intercourse rises to a remarkable and incomparable height in the relation of God to those He has chosen —to the prophets whom He will send out (Ex. 33, 12; Jer 1, 5), to Israel which He is preparing for its commission (Amos 3, 2; Hos. 13, 5), or simply to the simple and loyal men who trust in His protection alone (Nahum 1, 7; Ps. 31, 8; 37, 18). Through His contact with them God draws them out of the abundance of living creatures in order to communicate with them. This 'knowing' of His, this reaching out to touch and to grasp, means that the man is lifted out, and it is as those who have been lifted out that they have intercourse with

Him. In the verse of the Psalm of which I am speaking, however, there is something particular added, which is said only here, and it is this. The Psalm does not say that God knows the proven ones, the pious, but that He knows their way. The way, the way of life of these men is so created that at each of its stages they experience the divine contact afresh. And they experience it as befits a real way, at each stage they experience it in the manner specifically appropriate to the stage. Their experience of the divine 'knowing' is not like any experience of nature, it is a genuinely biographical experience, that is, what is experienced in this manner is experienced in the course of one's own personal life, in destiny as it is lived through in each particular occasion. However cruel and contrary this destiny might appear when viewed apart from intercourse with God, when it is irradiated by His 'knowing' it is 'success', just as every action of this man, his disappointments and even his failures, are success. O the happiness of the man who goes the way which is shown and 'known' by God!

The way is shown by God in his 'direction', the Torah. This God directs, that is, he teaches us to distinguish between the true way and the false ways. His direction, his teaching of the distinction, is given to us. But it is not enough to accept it. We must 'delight' in it, we must cling to it with a passion more exalted than all the passions of the wicked. Nor is it enough to learn it passively. We must again and again 'mutter' it, we must repeat its living word after it, with our speaking we must enter into the word's spokenness, so that it is spoken anew by us in our biographical situation of today —and so on and on in eternal actuality. He who in his own activity serves the God Who reveals Himself—even though he may by nature be sprung from a mean earthly realm—is transplanted by the streams of water of the Direction. Only now can his own being thrive, ripen and bring forth fruit, and the law by which seasons of greenness and seasons of withering succeed one another in the life of the living being, no longer holds for him —his sap circulates continually in undiminished freshness.

These, who are constant in the way of God, stand in contrast to those two other classes of men, the sinners and the wicked. It is essential to distinguish these two classes from one another. The parallelism in the form means here, as so often, not a mere correspondence but a completion. 'Wicked' here really describes a kind of man, a persistent

disposition, whereas 'sinners' describes rather a condition, a fit which from time to time attacks the
man, without adhering to him. Sinners again and
again miss God's way, the wicked oppose it in
accordance with the basic attitude of their constitution. The sinner does evil, the wicked man is evil.
That is why it is said only of the wicked, and not
of sinners, that their way peters out and that they
are like the chaff which a wind sweeps away. And
when it is said of the wicked as of the sinners that
they 'do not stand', there is a fundamental distinction. The wicked do not stand 'in the judgement',
while the sinners do not stand only 'in the congregation of the proven ones'. In the 'judgement' it
is existence which is at stake. Since the wicked man
has negated his existence he ends in nothing, his
way is his judgement. But with sinners it is different: their 'not standing' does not refer to the
decision of the supreme judgement, it is only a
human community which is unable to offer them
any stability if it is not to make its own stability
questionable. But entry into this community is not
closed to them. They need only to carry out that
turning into God's way, of which the Psalm permits
us to divine that it is not merely open to them
but that they themselves may desire it in the depths

59

of their heart, whereas they do not feel themselves strong enough, or rather fancy they are not strong enough, to enter upon it. Is the way, then, closed to the wicked? It is not closed from God's side—so we may continue the reflection of the Psalm—but it is closed from the side of the wicked themselves. For in distinction from the sinners they do not wish to be able to turn. That is why their way peters out.

Here, it is true, there arises for us modern interpreters of the Psalms the question to which neither this nor any other Psalm nor any human word knows the answer: how can an evil will exist, when God exists? The abyss which is opened by this question stretches, even more uncannily than the abyss of Job's question, into the darkness of the divine mystery. Before this abyss the interpreter of the Psalms stands silent.

IMAGES OF GOOD AND EVIL

Translated by
MICHAEL BULLOCK

The translator wishes to acknowledge Professor Buber's
kindness in checking the whole of the translation before
it went to press and making a number of valuable
suggestions.

PREFACE

In the *Entretiens de Pontigny*, founded and directed by my unforgettable friend Paul Desjardins, there was raised in the summer of 1935, in connection with a discussion of asceticism, the problem of evil. I had been preoccupied with this problem since my youth, but not until the year following the first World War had I approached it independently; since then I had repeatedly dealt with it in my writings and lectures, and it was the subject of my first lecture-course in the Science of Religion at the University of Frankfurt am Main. I therefore took an active part in the discussion, and the lively exchange of ideas, particularly with Nicolai Berdyaeff and Ernesto Buonaiuti, who have now also passed on, led me to renewed reflection upon what Berdyaeff termed this 'paradoxical' problem. In the *Entretiens* for the following year, in ten days of discussion devoted to just this problem, I set out my conception in greater detail; in so doing,

I drew a comparison between two historical viewpoints, the ancient Iranian and the Hebrew. I was concerned above all to show that in their anthropological[1] reality, that is, in the factual context of the life of the human person, good and evil are not, as they are usually thought to be, two structurally similar qualities situated at opposite poles, but two qualities of totally different structure. *Impossible de le résoudre,* Berdyaeff had said, *ni même de le poser de manière rationelle, parcequ'alors il disparaît.* And in direct conjunction with this 'impossibility' he posed the question of the point of attack for the struggle against evil. In answer to this consideration I now attempted in my lecture to give, in place of a 'solution' of the problem of evil, a synthetic description of evil happening, and so to assist in its understanding. I was able to give a considerably briefer and more precise reply to the question as to the point of attack for the struggle; it ran: The struggle must begin within one's own soul—all else will follow upon this.

This second answer I elaborated a few years later, already in Jerusalem, in the form of a novel, or more correctly, a chronicle, which I entitled

---

[1] I use the word 'anthropological' here entirely in the sense of modern philosophical anthropology; cf. the treatise 'What is Man?' in my book *Between Man and Man* (1947).

Gog and Magog.[1] Its central theme is contained in the following words of a disciple:

'Rabbi', he said in an almost failing voice, 'what is the nature of this Gog? He can exist in the outer world only because he exists within us?' He pointed to his own breast. 'The darkness out of which he was hewn needed to be taken from nowhere else than from our own slothful and malicious hearts. It is our betrayal of God that has made Gog to grow so great.'

Fully to understand this passage the reader must recall the time at which the novel was written.

Elaboration of my reply to Berdyaeff's indication of the 'impossibility of solution' had to wait for another decade. It is given in this book. It took so long to mature above all because it dawned on me only gradually that the Biblical myths of good and evil on the one hand, and the Avestic and post-Avestic on the other correspond with two fundamentally different kinds and stages of evil. In order to make clear their meaning, which transcends the

[1]First written by me in Hebrew, and later in German. First printed in the workers' paper *Davar*, January-October 1941; printed as a book in Hebrew, Jerusalem 1943; English translation by Ludwig Lewisohn under the title *For the Sake of Heaven*, Philadelphia 1945; German edition, Heidelberg 1949.

anthropological, I have preceded their description by an interpretation of the two groups of myths. We are dealing here, as Plato already knew, with truths such as can be communicated adequately to the generality of mankind only in the form of myths. The anthropological exposition shows the domain in which they materialize again and again. Everything conceptual in this connection is merely an aid, a useful bridge between myth and reality. Its construction is indispensable. Man knows of chaos and creation in the cosmogonic myth and he learns that chaos and creation take place in himself, but he does not see the former and the latter together; he listens to the myth of Lucifer and hushes it up in his own life. He needs the bridge.

PART ONE

I. THE TREE OF KNOWLEDGE

THE Biblical account of the so-called fall of man may well be founded upon a primeval myth of the envy and vengeance of gods, of whose contents we have no more than an inkling: the story that has been written down and preserved for us has acquired a very different meaning. The divine being whose actions are here recorded is repeatedly referred to (with the exception of the dialogue between the serpent and the woman) by an appellation, alien to the style of the rest of the Bible, which is compounded out of a proper name—interpreted elsewhere (Exodus 3, 14 f.) as He-is-there—and a generic term which is plural in form and corresponds most nearly to our 'Godhead'. This God is the sole possessor of the power both of creation and of destiny; he is surrounded by other celestial beings, but all these are subject to him and without names or power of their own. Of course, he does not impose his will upon man, the last of his works; he does not compel him, he only commands, or rather forbids him, albeit under a severe threat. The man—and with him his woman, who was not created till after the prohibition had been pronounced, but who appears to have become cognizant of it in some peculiar manner whilst still a rib within the body of the man— may give or withhold his obedience, for he is at liberty; they are both at liberty to accede to their creator or to refuse themselves to him. Yet their transgression of the prohibition is not reported to us as a decision between good and evil, but as something other, of whose otherness we must take account.

The terms of the dialogue with the serpent are already strange enough. It speaks as though it knew very imprecisely what it obviously knows very precisely. 'Indeed, God has said: You shall not eat of every tree of the garden . . .' it says and breaks off. Now the woman talks, but she too intensifies God's prohibition and adds to it words which he did not use: '. . . touch it not, else you must die.' As becomes manifest subsequently, the serpent is both right and wrong in denying that this will be the consequence: they do not have to die after eating, they merely plunge into *human* mortality, that is, into the knowledge of death to come—the serpent plays with the word of God, just as Eve played with it. And now the incident itself begins: the woman regards the tree. She does not merely see that it is a delight to the eye, she also sees in it that which cannot be seen: how good its fruit tastes and that it bestows the gift of understanding. This seeing has been explained as a metaphorical expression for perceiving, but how could these qualities of the tree be perceived? It must be a contemplation that is meant, but it is a strange, dreamlike kind of contemplation. And so, sunk in contemplation, the woman plucks, eats and hands to the man, and now he eats also, whose presence has till then been revealed to us by neither word nor gesture—she seems moved by dream-longing, but it seems to be truly in dream-lassitude that he takes and eats. The whole incident is spun out of play and dream; it is irony, a mysterious irony of the narrator, that spins it. It is apparent: the two doers know not what they do, more than this, they can only do it, they cannot know it. There is no room here for the pathos of the two principles, as we see it in the ancient Iranian religion, the pathos of the choice made by the Two themselves and by the whole of mankind after them.

And nevertheless both of them, good and evil, are to be found here—but in a strange, ironical shape, which the commentators have not understood as such and hence have not understood at all.

The tree of whose forbidden fruit the first humans eat is called the tree of the knowledge of good and evil; so does God himself also call it. The serpent promises that by partaking of it, they would become like God, knowers of good and evil; and God seems to confirm this when he subsequently says that they have thereby become 'as one of us', to know good and evil. This is the repetitive style of the Bible, the antitheses constantly reappear in fresh relationships with one another: its purpose is to demonstrate with superclarity that it is they we are dealing with. But nowhere is their meaning intimated. The words may denote the ethical antithesis, but they may also denote that of beneficial and injurious, or of delightful and repulsive; immediately after the serpent's speech the woman 'sees' that the tree is 'good to eat', and immediately upon God's prohibition followed his dictum that it was 'not good' that man should be alone—the adjective translated by 'evil' is equally indefinite.

In the main, throughout the ages, three interpretations have repeatedly emerged in explanation of what the first humans acquired by partaking of the fruit. One, which refers to the acquisition of sexual desire, is precluded both by the fact of the creation of man and woman as sexually mature beings and by the concept of 'becoming-like-God', which is coupled with the 'knowledge of good and evil': this God is supra-sexual. The other interpretation, relating to the acquisition of moral consciousness, is no less contrary to the nature of this God: we have only to think of the declaration in His mouth that man, now that he has acquired moral consciousness, must not be allowed to attain aeonian life as well! According to the third interpretation, the meaning of this 'knowledge of good and 'evil' is nothing else than: cognition in general, cognizance of the world, knowledge of all the good and bad things there are, for this would be in line with Biblical usage, in which the antithesis good and evil is often used to denote 'anything', 'all kinds of things'. But this interpretation, the favourite one today, is also unfounded. There is no place in the

71

Scriptures where the antithesis meant simply 'anything' or 'all kinds of things'; if all those passages which are taken as having this significance are examined in relation to the concrete nature of the current situation and the current intention of the speaker, they are always found to refer in actual fact to an affirmation or a negation of both good and bad, evil or ill, of both favourable and unfavourable. The 'be it . . . be it . . .', which is always found in this context, does not relate to the whole scale of that which is, inclusive of everything neutral, but precisely to the opposites and to discrimination between them, even though knowing them is bound up with knowing 'everything in the world.' Thus it is stated, for instance, as of the angel as the heavenly, so of the king as the earthly representative of God, that he knows all things (II Samuel 14, 20); but where it is said of him that he discerns the good and the evil (do. v. 17), this refers specifically to the knowledge of the right and the wrong, the guilty and the innocent, which the earthly judge, like the heavenly who rules over the nations (cf. Psalms 82, 2 and 58, 2), receives from his divine commissioner, so that he may give it practical realisation. But added to this is the fact that the word sequence 'good and evil' (without an article)—which, apart from our tale, only occurs on one other occasion, in a subsequent passage which is dependent upon this one (Deuteronomy 1, 39)—is given an emphasis in the story of Paradise, by repetition and other stylistic means, that does not permit us to suppose it a rhetorical flourish. Neither is it the case that 'cognition in general' only came to the first humans when they partook of the fruit: it is not before a creature without knowledge that, even before the creation of the woman, God brings the beasts that he may give them their appointed names, but before the bearer of his own breath, the being upon whom, at the very hour of creation, he had manifestly bestowed the abundance of knowledge contained in speech, of which that being is now the master.

'Knowledge of good and evil' means nothing else than: cognizance of the opposites which the early literature of mankind designated by these two terms; they still include the fortune and the misfortune or the order and the disorder which is experienced by a person, as well as that which he causes. This is still the same in the early Avestic texts, and it is the same in those of the Bible which precede written prophecy and to which ours belongs. In the terminology of modern thought, we

can transcribe what is meant as: adequate awareness of the opposites inherent in all being within
the world, and that, from the viewpoint of the
Biblical creation-belief, means: adequate awareness of the opposites latent in creation.

We can only reach complete understanding if
we remain fully aware that the basic conception
of all the theo- and anthropology of the Hebrews,
namely the immutable difference and distance
which exists between God and man, irrespective
of the primal fact of the latter's 'likeness' to God
and of the current fact of his 'nearness' to Him
(Psalm 73, 28), also applies to the knowledge of
good and evil. This knowledge as the primordial
possession of God and the same knowledge as the
magical attainment of man are worlds apart in their
nature. God knows the opposites of being, which
stem from His own act of creation; He encompasses
them, untouched by them; He is as absolutely
familiar with them as he is absolutely superior to
them; He has direct intercourse with them (this is
obviously the original meaning of the Hebrew verb
'know': be in direct contact with), and this in their
function as the opposite poles of the world's being.
For as such He created them—we may impute this
late Biblical doctrine (Isaiah, 45, 7) to our narra-

tor, in its elementary form. Thus He who is above all opposites has intercourse with the opposites of good and evil that are of His own making; and something of this His primordial familiarity with them He appears, as can be gathered from the words, 'one of us' (Genesis 3, 22), to have bestowed upon the 'sons of God' (6, 2) by virtue of their share in the work of creation. The 'knowledge' acquired by man through eating the miraculous fruit is of an essentially different kind. A superior-familiar encompassing of opposites is denied to him who, despite his 'likeness' to God, has a part only in that which is created and not in creation, is capable only of begetting and giving birth, not of creating. Good and evil, the yes-position and the no-position of existence, enter into his living cognizance; but in him they can never be temporally coexistent. He knows oppositeness only by his situation within it; and that means de facto (since the yes can present itself to the experience and perception of man in the no-position, but not the no in the yes-position): he knows it directly from within that 'evil' at times when he happens to be situated there; more exactly: he knows it when he recognises a condition in which he finds himself whenever he has transgressed the command of God, as the 'evil' and the one he has thereby lost and which, for the time being, is inaccessible to him, as the good. But at this point, the process in the human soul becomes a process in the world: through the recognition of oppositeness, the opposites which are always latently present in creation break out into actual reality, they become existent.

In just this manner the first humans, as soon as they have eaten of the fruit, 'know' that they are naked. 'And the eyes of both of them were opened': they see themselves as they are, but now since they see themselves so, not merely without clothing, but 'naked'. Recognition of this fact, the only recorded consequence of the magical partaking, cannot be adequately explained on the basis of sexuality, although without the latter it is, of course, inconceivable. Admittedly, they had not been ashamed before one another and now they are ashamed, not merely before one another, but with one another before God (3, 10), because, overcome by the knowledge of oppositeness, they feel the natural state of unclothedness, in which they find themselves, to be an ill or an evil, or rather both at once and more besides, and by this very feeling they make it so; but as a countermeasure they conceive, will and establish the 'good' of clothing. One is

ashamed of being as one is because one now 'recognises' this so-being in its oppositional nature as an
intended shall-be; but now it has really become a
matter for shame. In themselves, naturally, neither
the concept of clothed- and unclothedness, nor that
of man and woman before one another, have anything whatsoever to do with good and evil; human
'recognition' of opposites alone brings with it the
fact of their relatedness to good and evil. In this
lamentable effect of the great magic of the becoming-like-God the narrator's irony becomes apparent; an irony whose source was obviously great
suffering through the nature of man.

But does not God himself confirm that the serpent's promise has been fulfilled? He does; but this
most extreme expression, this pronouncement, 'Man
is become as one of us, to know good and evil', is
also still steeped in the ironic dialectic of the whole
which, it here shows most clearly, does not emanate
from an intention freely formed by the narrator,
but is imposed upon by him by the theme—which
corresponds exactly to his suffering through the
nature of man—at this stage of its development. Because man is now numbered amongst those who
know good and evil, God wishes to prevent him
from also eating of the tree of life and 'living by

aeons'. The narrator may have taken the motif from the ancient myth of the envy and vengeance of gods: if so, it acquired through him a meaning fundamentally different from its original one. Here there can no longer be any expression of fear that man might now become a match for the celestial beings: we have just seen how earthly is the nature of man's knowledge of 'good and evil'. The 'like one of us' can be uttered here only in the ironic dialectic. But now it is the irony of a 'divine compassion'.[1] God, who breathed his breath into the construction of dust, placed him in the garden of the four rivers and gave him a helpmate, wanted him to accept his continued guidance; he wanted to protect him from the opposites latent in existence. But man—caught up in demonry, which the narrator symbolizes for us with his web of play and dream—withdrew at once from both the will of God and from his protection and, though without properly understanding what he was doing, nevertheless with this deed, unrealised by his understanding, caused the latent opposites to break out at the most dangerous point, that of the world's closest proximity to God. From that moment on,

[1]Thus Procksch in his Commentary on Genesis, the only one, as far as I see, to give the correct interpretation here.

oppositeness takes hold of him, not indeed as a must-sin—of that, and hence of original sin, there is no question here—but as the ever-recrudescent reaction to the no-position and its irredeemable perspective; he will ever anew find himself naked and look around for fig leaves with which to plait himself a girdle. This situation would inevitably develop into full demonry, if no end were set to it. Lest the thoughtless creature, again without knowing what he is doing, should long for the fruit of the other tree and eat himself into aeons of suffering, God prevents his return to the garden from which he expelled him in punishment. For man as a 'living soul' (2, 7) known death is the threatening boundary; for him as the being driven round amidst opposites it may become a haven, the knowledge of which brings comfort.

This stern benefaction is preceded by the passing of sentence. It announces no radical alteration of that which already exists; it is only that all things are drawn into the atmosphere of oppositeness. When she gives birth, for which she was prepared at the time of her creation, woman shall suffer pains such as no other creature suffers—henceforth a price must be paid for being human; and the desire to become once more one body with the man (cf.

2, 24) shall render her dependent upon him. To the man work, which was already planned for him before he was set in the garden, shall become an affliction. But the curse conceals a blessing. From the *seat*, which had been made ready for him, man is sent out upon a *path*, his own, the human path. That this is the path into the world's history, that only through it does the world have a history—and an historical goal—must, in his own way, have been felt by the narrator.

II. KAIN

Upon the tale of the tree of knowledge follows in
the Scriptures that of fratricide, different from the
former in its style and the manner in which it is
conveyed, without irony and without lingering; a
brief, dry report, which has preserved archaic elements within it, but which, in its present linguistic
version, is unmistakably linked up with the former.
It and not the former is the story of the first
'iniquity' (4, 13) in the universal human sense, that
is of one which if, as here, it took place within the
clan, would always be punished as such in every
society known to us. The former describes an action
which earns punishment, not of itself, but as disobedience, the latter a deed which is wrong by its
very nature. However it may have been fashioned
and intended in its original and independent form,
only its combination with the tale of the eating of
the forbidden fruit drew out of it an immense significance: this, we are now told, is how accom-

81

plished human 'knowledge of good and evil' works out in the generations that come after—not indeed as 'original sin', but as the specific sin, only possible in relation to God, which alone makes possible general sin against the fellow-man and hence, of course, once more against God as his guardian (II Samuel 12, 13). The deed of the first humans belonged to the sphere of pre-evil, Kain's deed to that of evil, which only came into being as such through the act of knowledge. We who have been born late and are concerned to know that knowledge and at the same time to prevail over it, must stress the perspective founded on the combination of the two tales.

The first thing we learn about the couple that was driven out of Paradise is that the man 'knew' his woman (4, 11). With this word the prehistoric genealogists designate the sexual acts of Adam and Kain only (vv. 17 and 25); it may be assumed that the designation is intended to keep us in the atmosphere of that first 'knowing'; not as if something from that sundered polarity attached itself to the sexual act as such, but *now* it takes place between those who have known, so that something from this enters into their knowing of each other. A discrimination between unhallowed copulation, repugnant to God—in which, the first humans' sin is supposed to have consisted—and that which is hallowed and acceptable to God has been incorrectly ascribed to the tale of the 'fall of man' by ancient and modern exegetists; there is no foundation here for distinctions of this kind, and there is equally little ground to assume that marital relations between Adam and Eve only began after the expulsion. But in the manner the Hebrew Bible has of expressing some things, not directly, but only by the selection of particular words, it is hinted here that their post-Paradisal intimacy was no longer the same as the Paradisal, that it had become cognizant, and that means exposed to the opposites inherent in all existence within the world, through awareness of them.

It is precisely from this first post-Paradisal copulation that the first son of man springs, and he is the first man to become guilty in the exact human sense. But it is just at his birth that the Scriptures put into the mouth of the child's mother, in explanation of the name she gives him, a pronouncement, singular and unlike all other maternal pronouncements in the Bible. She says she has 'brought forth' a manchild with YHVH; for that is the original meaning of the verb, as can be seen both from other passages in the Bible and, in particular, from the language of the North Syrian epic, which is cognate with Hebrew, where the mother of the gods is called by the same word, as their 'bringer forth', that is used here by the 'mother of all living' (3, 20). This is manifestly connected with the idea that the process of the first birth is only made possible by special divine intervention, presumably at the time of the initial labour-pains, for which reason also every firstborn of man and beast, as the 'breaking open of the womb' (Exodus 13, 12, 15; 34, 19; Numbers 3, 12; 18, 15), belongs to God. But only here is it directly indicated that God himself assists a firstborn into the world, and just this firstborn is the first murderer. The belief, not formulated conceptually till a late date, that God set man in the world as a primordially free being has here found its strangest and most fearful expression.

Kain and his brother now face one another in a sacrificial rite; Kain, the husbandman, brings the fruits of the ground; he is followed by the shepherd with the firstlings of the flock. God regards the latter offering with favour, but not the former. Because he is more favourably disposed towards the cattle-breeder than towards the man of the soil? Nothing permits this assumption. The fact that a curse has been laid upon the tilled soil can also

scarcely be determinant here; the author undoubtedly knew the daily offering of the 'bread of the
face', which makes its appearance at an early age
(I Samuel 21, 7). A more likely consideration is the
fact that in Semitic religions we frequently find the
self-offering which in decisive hours is properly incumbent upon the head of the clan or tribe, com-
muted to an animal-, never to a plant-sacrifice. But
neither can this be regarded as the central motive
here, since nothing points to it. The initial manifest
implication is rather that God sees Kain does not
'purpose good' (v. 7). But with this something yet
more important is connected. What we have before
us here seems to me an example of that uncanny
occurrence which the Scriptures themselves understand as divine temptation. This name is first given
to the third of these actions of God, more radical
and more positive than the two preceding it and,
contrary to them, also radically positive in out-
come, but even more uncanny than they are; the
command to Abraham to sacrifice his son (22, 1).
The settlement beside the forbidden tree is also a
temptation, but one which is *not* withstood, and
another such is the disregard of Kain's offering.

God now enters into conversation with the man
inflamed with wrath, whose countenance has 'fallen'

or 'sunken', as he did with the first humans after their sin; such dialogues are the great respirations of Biblical narration. What he says to Kain consists of an introductory question and a pronouncement which apparently—if it is not regarded, as it is by many commentators, as corrupt—stems for the most part (ten words out of fifteen) from an earlier tradition and bears an archaic character, whereas the concluding residue is patently intended to stress the connection with the tale of Paradise. The whole of God's speech can only be translated conjecturally, the most likely version being: 'Why art thou wroth? Why is thy countenance fallen? Is it not so: if thou purposest good, bear it aloft, but if thou dost not purpose good—sin before the door, a beast lying in wait, unto thee his desire, but prevail thou over him'. This is the first occurrence of the word, which is absent from the tale of the Fall, the word 'sin', and here it is apparently the name of a demon who, by nature a 'beast that lies in wait', at times lurks on watch at the entrance to a soul that does not purpose good, to see if it will fall prey to him, that soul within whose power it still lies to over-power him. If the passage may be so understood, it is the truest example within the world's early epic literature of a divine being's appeal to men to decide for the 'good', that means to set out in the direction of the divine.

It is, however, of fundamental importance to comprehension to differentiate precisely between the two stages or strata which are here involved. Our initial position is, so to speak, in the forecourt of the soul. Here, with absolute clarity, there is, as it were, a static opposition, reminiscent of the Avestic opposition of 'goodness of mind' and 'badness of mind': a distinction is made between a state of the soul in which it purposes good and one in which it does not, in fact therefore, not between a good and an ungood 'disposition', but between a disposition to good and its absence. Not until we deal with this second state, with the lack of direction towards God, do we penetrate to the chamber of the soul at whose entrance we encounter the demon. Not till then are we dealing with the true dynamic of the soul as it is given by the 'knowledge of good and evil', and by man's self-exposure to the opposites inherent in existence within the world, but now in its ethical mould. From quite general opposites, embracing good and evil as well as good and ill and good and bad, we have arrived at the circumscribed area peculiar to man, in which only good and evil still confront each other. It is peculiar to man—so may we late-comers formulate it—because it can only be perceived introspectively, can only be recognised in the conduct of the soul towards itself: a man only knows factually what 'evil' is insofar as he knows about himself, everything else to which he gives this name is merely mirrored illusion; but self-perception and self-relationship are the peculiarly human, the irruption of a strange element into nature, the inner lot of man. Here also, then, the demoniac, whose desire is towards us, as a woman's is towards a man—to arouse this association in the reader, one of the phrases God addressed to Eve is incorporated in his speech to Kain—is first to be encountered directly; from this point too it first becomes accessible and demonstrable to us in the world. Here, at the inner threshold, there is of course no further room for disposition; the struggle must now be fought out.

In contradistinction to the first humans, Kain does not reply to God's address, he refuses to account to him for this deed. He refuses to face the demon at the threshold; he thus delivers himself up to the latter's 'desire'. Intensification and confirmation of indecision is decision to evil.

So Kain murders. He speaks to his brother, we are not told what he says; he goes with him into the field; he strikes him dead. . . Why? No motive, not even jealousy, is sufficient to explain the monstrous deed. We must remember that it is the first murder: Kain does not yet know that such a thing exists, that one can murder, that if one strikes a person hard enough one strikes him dead. He does not yet know what death and killing are. It is not a motive that is decisive, but an occasion. In the vortex of indecision Kain strikes out, at the point of greatest provocation and least resistance. He does not murder, he has murdered.

When God's curse—again in words which refer back to the cursing of the first humans and lead over and beyond it—sends him forth from the ploughed fields to be 'a fugitive and a vagabond on earth', he is allotting him a destiny which is the incarnate representation of what took place within his soul.

III. IMAGINATION AND IMPULSE

THE Biblical tale of the flood is framed by two sentences in similar language, but of disparate content, which require to be understood in reference to one another. One (Genesis 6, 5) makes God see 'that the wickedness of man is great on earth and all the imagery of the designs of his heart only evil the whole day', and he repents of having made man. In the second (8, 21), God himself speaks: he does not wish again to curse the earth on account of man, 'for the imagery of man's heart is evil from his youth'.

'And YHVH saw': here the narrator is obviously looking back upon that sevenfold 'And God saw' of the creation story. Six times God sees 'that it is good', but the seventh time, after the creation of man, he looks at everything he has made and sees 'that it is very good'. How did the first humans' very good become the only-evil of the human race?

But it is not man who is seen as evil. The

'wickedness' does not imply a corruption of the soul, the living soul which was breathed into man, but of the 'way' (6, 12), which fills the earth with 'violence' (v. 11)—and this results from the intervention, not of the evil soul, but of the evil 'imagery'. The wickedness of the actions is derived from its, the imagery's, wickedness.

Imagery or 'imaging' corresponds, in a conceptual world which is simpler but more powerful than ours, to our 'imagination'—not the power of imagination, but its products. Man's heart designs designs in images of the possible, which could be made into the real. Imagery, 'the depictions of the heart' (Psalm 73, 7), is play with possibility, play as self-temptation, from which ever and again violence springs. It too, like the deed of the first humans, does not proceed from a decision; but the place of the real, perceived fruit has been taken by a possible, devised, fabricated one which, however, can be made, could be made—is made into a real one. This imagery of the possible, and in this its nature, is called evil. Good is not devised; the former is evil because it distracts from divine reality.

The change against the situation of the first humans stems from the knowledge of good and evil,

not from disobedience as such, but from its immediate consequences. Man has therein become 'like
God', in that now, like him, he 'knows' oppositeness; but he cannot, like God, rise superior to it.
Thus, from divine reality, which was allotted to
him, from the 'good' actuality of creation, he is
driven out into the boundless possible, which he
fills with his imaging, that is evil because it is ficti-
tious: even in exile, man's expulsion from divine
reality is continually repeated by his own agency.
In the swirling space of images, through which he
strays, each and every thing entices him to be made
incarnate by him; he grasps at them like a wanton
burglar, not with decision, but only in order to
overcome the tension of omnipossibility; it all becomes reality, though no longer divine but his, his
capriciously constructed, indestinate reality, his violence, which overcomes him, his handiwork and
fate.

That man, at the mercy of the knowledge of
good and evil, without being able to transcend its
opposites—there is no other transcendence than that
of the Creator—brings the compelled chaotic of the
possible, which is continuously, capriciously incar-
nating itself, over the created world, that is what
causes God to repent of having made man; he

wants to 'wipe him out from the face of the earth' and with him every living thing drawn by the author of violence into his corruption—it repents him that he made them all (6, 7).

But in exactly the same language, with the most forceful reference back to what has been reported thus, God—after the work of destruction—explains his forgiveness, his resolution never again to strike the living thing he had made, precisely on the grounds that 'the imagery of man's heart is evil from his youth'. No longer 'all the imagery', no longer 'only evil', and curiously added afresh 'from his youth'. It is not to be understood in any other manner than that God deliberates: imagination is not entirely evil, it is evil and good, for in the midst of it and from out of it decision can arouse the heart's willing direction toward him, master the vortex of possibility and realize the human figure purposed in the creation, as it could not yet do prior to the knowledge of good and evil. For straying and caprice are not innate in man, they are not of the nature of original sin; in spite of all the burdens of past generations, he always begins anew as a person, and the storm of adolescence first deluges him with the infinitude of the possible— greatest danger and greatest opportunity at once.

This was the point at which, several hundred years later, the Talmudic doctrine of the two urges started. It found the word *yetser*, which I have rendered by 'imagery', already transformed in meaning; as early as Jesus Sirach it signifies the own impulse, into whose hand created man is given by God, but with liberty to keep commandment and faith in order to do the will of God. In the Talmud, the concept, under the influence of increasing reflection, is partly split up into a 'good' and a 'evil' urge and partly used, without any attribute, to designate the second of these as the elemental one.

In the creation of man, the two urges are set in opposition to each other. The Creator gives them to man as his two servants which, however, can only accomplish their service in genuine collaboration. The 'evil urge' is no less necessary than its companion, indeed even more necessary than it, for without it man would woo no woman and beget no children, build no house and engage in no economic activity, for it is true that 'all travail and all skill in work is the rivalry of a man with his neighbour' (Ecclesiastes 4, 4). Hence this urge is called 'the yeast in the dough,' the ferment placed in the soul by God, without which the human dough does not rise.

Thus, a man's status is necessarily bound up with the volume of 'yeast' within him; 'whoever is greater than another, his urge is greater than the other's.' The high value of the 'evil urge' finds its strongest expression in an interpretation of the scriptural verse (Genesis 1, 31) which asserts that God, on the evening of the day on which he had created man, looked upon all he had made and found it 'very good': this 'very good' applies to the evil urge, whereas the good one only earns the predicate 'good'; of the two, it is the evil urge which is fundamental. But that it is called the evil urge derives from man's having made it so. Thus Kain (as is said in the Midrash) might indeed respond to the God who was calling him to account that it was He, God, Himself who had implanted in him the evil urge; but the rejoinder would be untrue, since only through him, man, did it become evil. It became so, and continually becomes so, because man separates it from its companion and in this condition of independence makes an idol of precisely that which was intended to serve him. Man's task, therefore, is not to extirpate the evil urge, but to reunite it with the good. David, who did not dare to stand up to it and therefore 'slew' it in himself—as it runs in one of his Psalms

(109, 22): 'My heart is pierced through within me' —did not fulfil it, but Abraham, whose *whole* heart was found faithful before God, who now made a covenant with him (Nehemiah 9, 8),[1] did. Man is bidden (Deuteronomy 6, 5): 'Love the Lord with all thine heart,' and that means, with thy two united urges. The evil urge must also be included in the love of God thus and thus only does it become perfect, and thus and thus only does man become once more as he was created: 'very good.' To achieve this, however, man must begin by harnessing both urges together in the service of God. As when a peasant possesses two oxen, one that has already ploughed and one that has not yet ploughed, and now a new field is to be cultivated: he brings both of them together beneath the yoke. But how is the evil urge to be prevailed upon to permit this to happen to it? Why, it is nothing but a crude ore, which must be placed in the fire in order to be moulded: so let it be totally immersed in the great fire of the Tora. And that also man cannot do of his own strength; we must pray to God to aid us to do His will with all our hearts.

[1]That the reduplicated form of the word for heart (*lebab* instead of *leb*) stands in the Scriptural verse, is explained by the unity of the heart, re-established by the unification of the urges.

Therefore the Psalmist beseeches (86, 11): 'Unite my heart to fear thy name'; for fear is the gateway to love.

This important doctrine cannot be understood as long as good and evil are conceived, as they usually are, as two diametrically opposite forces or directions. Its meaning is not revealed to us until we recognize them as similar in nature, the evil 'urge' as passion, that is, the power peculiar to man, without which he can neither beget nor bring forth, but which, left to itself, remains without direction and leads astray, and the 'good urge' as pure direction, in other words, as an unconditional direction, that towards God. To unite the two urges implies: to equip the absolute potency of passion with the one direction that renders it capable of great love and of great service. Thus and not otherwise can man become whole.

PART TWO

I. THE PRIMAL PRINCIPLES

IN the most ancient part of the Avesta, the hymnlike speeches and discourses of Zarathustra, we read of the two primal moving spirits: the good, good in disposition, in word and in work, and the evil, evil in disposition, in word and in work. 'Twins through sleep' they were, 'as was heard', that is, erstwhile sleeping companions in the womb of their origin. But then they were in opposition to one another, and the benignant spirit spoke to the wicked one: 'Neither our sentiments nor our judgments, neither our inclinations nor our intentions, neither our words nor our works, neither our selves nor our souls are in concord'. And they further established, confronting each other, life and death together, and that ultimately for the adherents of deception there exists the most evil, but for the adherents of truth the best disposition. So the two spirits then chose: the deceitful one chose

to do that which is most evil, but the most benignant spirit, he who is clad in the hardest heavens, chose being-true.

As nowhere else in the early literature of the
human race preserved to us, good and evil as principia are here brought together and put asunder.
They came forth from a primary initial community,
as 'twins'. From what seed and womb they stem is
not told us, but another time we hear that the
highest god, Ahura Mazdah, the 'Wise Lord', is the
father of the benignant spirit. So the two primal
opposites proceeded from him. Of a mother by
whose participation the contradiction could be explained we learn nothing. The god indeed surrounds himself with good powers, makes them battle with the evil ones and will make them conquer
the latter, but the opposite he is warring against
was manifestly encompassed by himself and he put
it out from himself into the being of the principia.
It is as though he has first to discard evil in order
to be able to subdue it. If, with the confrontation
of the twins, creation which is effected through
them is to commence, then the god before creation is the not-yet-good one; but in the creation the
god become good strives with that which he has

cast out from himself. Thus understood, God's primal act is a decision within himself, a primal choice, therefore, between still companionate good and evil, which prepares and makes possible their elected actions: the self-choice of good, which first renders it effectual and factual good, and the self-choice of evil, which renders it effectual and factual evil. But the primal choice is not directed towards creation, the latter being done for the sake of the 'turning point' at the end of the struggle.

Created man is ordained into the struggle for salvation as one who is himself called upon to choose between good and evil. Since the Wise Lord, creating by his spirit made man's life incarnate, the power of decision was entrusted to man. With a choice his *daena*, his self, embarked upon the earthly path; but ever anew must he, confronted by fresh interminglings of deception and truth, divide and decide. He must be aided from above: 'because the better path does not stand open to choice', says Zarathustra, 'I come to you all that we may live according to the truth'; his task is 'to place men before the choice' and show them the right path, so that, as the verse concerning the twins concludes, they may of their own decision accede to the Wise Lord with works of truth. Those who do so assist him 'to bring this existence to transfiguration'.

Like the God of heaven, man makes in himself the choice between good and evil, both of which, like Him, he bears within himself. Between God and man, however, stand the primal spirits, they too choosing, but in pure paradox. They neither contain nor confront a duplicity, each possesses only himself in the most extreme differentiation; the other one, the other thing, he only has as his absolute counterpart; such is the situation in which he chooses himself, his own kind and the work commensurate with it. Choosing, each acknowledges himself. The evil chooses and acknowledges himself, not however merely as created thus and not otherwise, but precisely as the evil, and for his followers he does not merely posit that after death they shall abide with him, but that it is just the worst existence which shall fall to their lot (in this doctrine there is no distinction of category between bad and evil: the bad is precisely that which causes evil, and in the last analysis there is no other evil than that which it causes). He desires evil as such; and thereby he fulfils the will of the highest god, who brought forth him and his twin: only through mastering unmitigated evil does existence attain to transfiguration.

Here the most harassing of questions remains unasked: how can the God of heaven, the primal being, have contained and encompassed evil? Around the Zarathustrian doctrine, which resists it, the question grows and grows, till the West Iranian religion develops the myth of Zurvan, Time Unbounded, in reply. We only know it from a later version, but its original content is unmistakable. Zurvan arises out of the primal sleep, as it seems, and sacrifices murmuring (the song of the generation of the gods, of which we know through Herodotus, is presumably meant), for a thousand or ten thousand years, to obtain the son, Ahura Mazdah, who would create heaven and earth. It would be beside the point to ask to whom he is sacrificing: similarly without recipient, the primeval Indian gods also sacrifice (or sacrifice themselves) that out of them may arise the world. After all the vain sacrifice, Zurvan is overcome by doubt: 'What avails sacrifice? Perhaps being is not?' Then arose two in the womb: the Wise Lord from the sacrifice, from the doubt the Wicked Spirit. But Zurvan is obviously a bisexual deity. Evil arises in him through his Fall. He does not choose, he doubts. Doubt is unchoice, indecision. Out of it arises evil.

We must note that the Wicked Spirit, Angra Mainyu, the well-known Ahriman, is here not the son of Ahura Mazdah, but his brother; Ahura Mazdah, Ormuzd, is, however, no longer a primal god, he enters at the beginning into being, and now precisely as the Only-good One. Thus here too the twins stand in radical antithesis to one another, but here, in contradistinction to the twin-myth of the Avesta, the antithesis of the one to the other is not explicitly stated, nor is the coming world-process between the two of them announced; we hear nothing of good and evil and their mutual relationship; we merely watch the appearance of the protagonists in the nascent cosmic conflict. Yet by what is recounted of the primal god himself we are led not less deep than there, and perhaps deeper, into the sphere of the question what good and evil are. There it was deception and truth, deception in the sense of being deceptive, truth in the sense of being true, which confronted one another; here doubt of being is the evil, the good is 'knowledge', belief in being, against which Zurvan transgresses. Here it is ultimately a question of fidelity and infidelity to being.

But some within the Zurvan community could not tolerate the notion of a divine Fall. Of these, some supposed that the time-god had gone astray as to being at a particular moment, but that from the beginning something bad, either bad thinking or a corruption of essence, had been admixed into him, and from this evil made its start; these are evidently reverting to the Avestic doctrine, though in a modified form. But others said Zurvan brought forth both, in order to mingle good with evil, from which it is clearly inferred that only through the gradated abundance of such inter-mixtures can the full manifoldness of things arise; here the fundament of the Iranian tradition is abandoned: good and evil are no longer irreconcilable principia, but utilisable qualities, before whose utilisability the question of an absolute worth and worthlessness vanishes. The fundament of another tradition is adopted, when in the opinion of a third of these sects Ahriman 'is an outcast angel who was cursed for his disobedience'. 'About that', so ends the report in this connection, 'much can be said'.

But there is a fragment of the Avesta which

runs: 'All good thoughts, all good words, all good deeds, I do consciously. All evil thoughts, all evil words, all evil deeds, I do unconsciously'. From here a path leads to the *psychological* problem of evil, as it first evolved in early Christendom.

II. THE LIE AGAINST BEING

In very various strata of Iranian literature from the most ancient texts of the Avesta to the poetry of Firdusi, we find elements of the saga of the primeval king Yima or Yama, a figure transmuted from primeval Indo-Aryan tradition into Indian and Iranian mythology. He 'whose gaze is like the sun', the 'great shepherd'—he has rightly been explained as the ancient shepherd-god of the Persians seen through the eyes of the peasant—is born immortal, but become mortal through his offence. The highest god, Ahura Mazdah, invites him to tend and protect religion, his, Ahura Mazdah's religion, and then, when Yima has declared himself unfit for this, he bids him foster, multiply and guard the world, his, Ahura Mazdah's world. This Yima is prepared to do; he assumes dominion over the world and it shall be a world in which none of the destructive powers will have a part, neither cold nor hot wind, nor sickness, nor death. Already previously he had besought the gods with sacrifices to grant him that in his realm man and cattle should be released from death, and water and trees from drought. He besought them to let him become the ruler of all countries, but above all lord of the demons who by crushing them shall take all evil from off Ahura Mazdah's creatures. This is now granted him. Three hundred years elapse, and since none of the creatures dies the earth overflows 'with small cattle and great cattle and dogs and birds and red flaming fires'. Called by Ahura Mazdah, Yima advances 'to the light, at midday, towards the path of the sun' and, with the gold-embellished goad and friendly incantation received from the god, urges on the earth to stretch apart until it has become greater by a third of its size. This is repeated twice more: the earth has now increased to double its size, and all creatures live upon it at their pleasure. But now Ahura Mazdah gathers together the gods and the best men, Yima at their peak. To him he announces that upon the world given over to materiality (here it sounds as though, in consequence of Yima's refusal, it was devoid of spirituality) there will descend the great winter, which will first cover it in snow and then flood it in the thaw, so that no creature will be able any more to put its feet upon

108

the ground. Then Yima is instructed to erect a mighty pen, like a citadel, and to secure therein the seed of the best and most beautiful of all living and growing things. It is done. Then, however, Yima vouchsafes the access of demonry, which he had hitherto held in coercion, and takes the lie into his mind by lauding and blessing himself. Immediately the regal glory, the lustre of good-fortune, which has till then irradiated his brow, leaves him in the shape of a raven, and he becomes mortal. He must wander without peace over the earth and time and again go into hiding. He joins forces with the demons and espouses a witch, with whom he begets all kinds of monsters. His sister disguises herself as the witch and lies with him. We do not learn what now takes place, but apparently the demons treat him as a rebel, for in the end he is sawn in pieces by them with a thousand-toothed saw. He is (as also in the early Indian songs, where he appears as the king of the dead) the first of those who have died; only after him do the rest die.

Many investigators find it incomprehensible, and hence unauthentic, that Yima's fault, which brought about his downfall, should have consisted in a lie. His *hubris* and self-adoration are taken to be a late motive, which, moreover, do not provide an adequate explanation of that lie. In fact we only find them in later and late texts; but their linking up with the lie goes back to very ancient associations, as when, in the great inscription of Darius, the arrogant rebel is designated a 'liar'. That the primeval king begins to laud and bless himself is not merely correctly designated a lie: it refers in fact to the primal lie of him who has been set over mankind, indeed to that of humanity as a whole, which ascribes the conquest of the powers of nature to its own superpower. It is no verbal lie confronting a verbal truth; it is an existential lie against being. Yima had entreated the Godhead that he should become immortal and to make every living thing immortal; he had prayed that he might become the master of the demons, and that he became. But now he avers that what was only vouchsafed to him he had done himself; he sees himself as a self-creator, through himself immortal and immortalizing, sees it as self-established self-grandeur that he held sway over the demons; he now lives and acts according to this viewpoint; he thus commits, as it has been put,[1] 'the inner untruth against God and himself', more exactly: he

[1]Lommel: *Zarathustra's Religion* (1930) 46.

commits with his existence the lie against being.

To become adequately aware of the existential profundity of the transition of a primordial being from truth to lie recounted here, we must look at it within the world-conflict between the two principles. For truth and lie are the two basic attitudes, or rather basic qualities, in whose opposition the opposition of the principles, good and evil, is represented. Only account must be taken of the fact that here truth implies something other than conscious concordance, and lie something other than conscious non-concordance between a thing asseverated and a real thing. The identical term lie is used in the Vedas, at times, to designate the uncanny game of hide-and-seek in the obscurity of the soul, in which it, the single human soul, evades itself, avoids itself, hides from itself. This lie in the own being now breaks out into the relationship to other souls, in that to worldly reality, in that to the divine. In the Avesta it is initially a breach of faith (lying to the contract-protecting deity Mithra means breaking the contract), then the falsification of a situation by the attitude, indeed the quality, of the person placed in it. The attitude refers back to the quality, but this latter is in no way a final, irreducible fact, but stems from the choice between truth and lie which is again and again, temporally and timelessly made and to be made by the essence of the person at the beginning of the way and in decisive hours, the choice, to express it existentially, between being-true and being-false. Being-true, however, ultimately signifies: strengthening, covering and confirming being at the point of one's own existence, and being-false ultimately signifies: weakening, desecrating and dispossessing being at the point of one's own existence. He who prefers the lie to the truth and chooses it instead of truth, intervenes directly with his decision into the decisions of the world-conflict. But this takes effect in the very first instance at just his point of being: since he gave himself over to the being-lie, that is to non-being, which passes itself off as being, he falls a victim to it. Thus Yima, the lord of the demons, falls into their power, since he crosses over from being-true to being-false; he becomes first their companion, then their victim. He effects factually a downfall of being: at precisely that point which is called Yima.

According to Augustine, whose heart was singed by a later gust of the burning wind of the Zarathustrian doctrine, truth and lie do not allude to the truth and falsehood of things themselves, but to a pronouncement of the soul. The soul pledges itself to the truth or to the lie. Human truth is a verification by man's being true.

PART THREE

I. THE TRUTH OF THE MYTHS

I N the two foregoing parts I have set out images made by an earlier humanity to depict the antithesis of good and evil or, more precisely, of evil in its contradictinction to good. Their purpose is certainly to recount the origin, or rather origins, of evil, but over and beyond the fulfilment of this purpose they give us representations of the structure of evil and this, naturally, in such a manner as to present us at the same time with indications of the nature of good. But they concern us here insofar, and only insofar, as they are *true* representations, insofar, therefore, as they can be of real assistance to us in attaining the necessary insight into the nature of evil and its relation to good. The mythical has entered into this our field of vision by virture of the truth of the myths. This cannot, of course, imply that a truth which once existed in non-mythical form has been 'decked out' as myth. It implies that the experience which has taken place (not 'been gained') in factual encounters with evil in the world and the soul is directly embodied in myth, without making the detour through conceptual or semi-conceptual determinations. But, in addition, it is necessary for us, after passing through all the allegories and mystosophies, unscientific and scientific, of myth-interpretation, to be able and willing to accept the facts concerning human reality which are offered to us in the realm of myth. Human reality, for our subject that means: what specifically happens in the life and soul of the man preoccupied with 'evil' and, particularly, of him who is on the point of falling victim to it.

In saying this I have also stated the precondition which we make and must make in order to learn from the myths what they are able to teach us about our subject. They tell us of the human constitution and movement of evil; but if we are to accord their account that manner of belief which is indispensable to its correct interpretation in our sense, in the sense of an apprehension of the subject itself, we must assume with them that such a specific dynamic structure really exists. In spite of

116

all the problematics of moral judgement, in spite of the constitutive impermanence of moral valuations, we must recognise and accept that in human reality there does indeed exist a specific of this kind, a specific, not according to valuation and judgement, but in being itself, and that this specificity is evidenced precisely in the fact that there things happen differently than otherwise in the life and the soul of man. It would, therefore, be totally insufficient to refer the matter to the existence of states whose nature and course are influenced by the 'moral censorship' of society, whether this censorship is the cause of submission or of rebellion; there can be no question at all here of the psychology of 'inhibitions' and 'repressions', which operate no less against some social convention or other than when it is a matter of that which is felt to be evil in the full meaning of the word. We must rather seek out this feeling itself in our experience of ourselves, where its differentiation from every other state of the soul is unmistakable, where, indeed, this psychological differentiation forcefully enjoins us to enquire as to the existence of an ontological one. It is of this latter that the mythos tells us latecomers of the spirit, who have outgrown it but are accessible to it. Nothing but our own experience of this enjoinder of the psychological singularity to enquire after the ontological can render us capable of receiving from mythos its most costly gift, the truth which it alone can express, and making it our own by interpreting it aright. We are competent to interpret the myths of the origin of evil only by virtue of our personal experience of it, but they alone lend it the character of truth. Only out of the conjunction of these two, primordial mythic intuition and directly experienced reality, does the light of the legitimate concept arise for this sphere too, probably the most obscure of all.

The myths recounted here stem from two historical fields: those of Part One, which tell of a slipping and falling into evil, from the Israelite accounts of the dawn of man; those of Part Two which deal with an entry or descent into evil, from the Ancient Iranian literature concerning the beginnings of divine and human decision for the No. This, however, in no way implies that in the Old Testament the first of these two conceptions was dominant. The story of the revolt of the race of men which sprang up again after the Flood, who built themselves a tower in order to make a great magic (a great 'name' action) against heaven, recalls the legend of Yima's rebellion, and very definitely the traditions, preserved in the sayings of the prophets, of the foolhardy angels—Lucifer, son of the dawn (Isaiah 14), and the great cherub (Ezekiel 28)— who, like Yima, imagined themselves godlike and were cast down. And again and again in the Old Testament, as in the Avesta and the texts dependent upon it, good and evil appear as alternative paths, before which man stands to choose between them, and that means (Deuteronomy 30, 19) between life and death; in both places we breathe the harsh air of decision. On the other hand, as we see, the Iranian doctrine of the genesis of the opposites out of a primal decision changes, at several points, into one of their genesis out of a primal doubt of the all-embracing Godhead. Gradually, however, a quite different doctrine develops from this, whose ultimate and extreme expression is Manichæism, according to which the antithesis of the two principles did not arise out of a primal act, but is eternal. The two fundamental types of evil from indecision and evil from decision are, therefore, not to be understood as having an ethnic basis.

But how can these two apparently mutually exclusive aspects, one of which shows us evil as an occurrence, the other as a deed, together teach us truth concerning the dynamic constitution of evil in the reality of human life? Only in the event of the contradiction between them being an apparent one; if, in fact, they are supplementary to one another. And such is the case. They are not supplementary to each other in the manner of the two sides of an object, this assumption would clearly be inappropriate here, but rather in the manner of the two stages or steps of a process. The Biblical stories allude to the first, the Iranian to the second stage; in this connection, however, we must keep in sight the fact that the process need not necessarily go further than the first stage.

If in the first image of the first series, the motif of becoming-like-God rings out strongly, but is brought to an ironic conclusion, whereas the same motif, merely transformed into being-like-God, dominates the scene in the las⁺ image of the second series, this is an indication to us that it is of especial significance to the whole process.

II. OUR POINT OF DEPARTURE

IT is usual to think of good and evil as two poles, two opposite directions, the two arms of a signpost pointing to right and left; they are understood as belonging to the same plane of being, as the same in nature, but the antithesis of one another. If we are to have in mind, not ethical abstractions, but existent states of human reality, we must begin by doing away with this convention and recognising the fundamental dissimilarity between the two in nature, structure and dynamics within human reality.

It is advisable to begin with evil, since, as will be shown, at the original stage, with which we shall deal first, the existent state of good in a certain matter presupposes that of evil. Now the latter, however, though concretely presented to extraspective vision also, in its actions and effects, its attitudes and behaviour, is presented in its essential state to our introspection only; and only our self-

knowledge—which of course, everywhere and always requires to be supplemented by our cognizance of the self-knowledge of others—is capable
of stating what happens when we do evil (only we
are wont to make far too little use of this self-
knowledge when we look around in the circles of
evil and are, at the same time, making some at-
tempt to understand it). Since, on the other hand,
such experience must have reached a high degree
of objectivity to be capable of providing us with
a knowledge of the subject, it is necessary to proceed from the viewpoint of a man looking back
over his life, who has achieved the indispensable
distance from even those amongst the remembered
inner and outer occurrences which, for him, are
bound up with the actuality of evil, but whose
memory has not lost the no less requisite force and
freshness. It follows from the foregoing that he
must now be aware of the existent actuality of evil
as evil, and that it is this which must be a specifically serious matter for him. Whoever has learnt to
dispose of the matter to his own satisfaction within
the more or less dubious sphere of so-called values,
for whom guilt is merely the civilized term for *tabu*,
to which corresponds no other reality than the con-
trol exercised by society and, attendant upon it, of

the 'super-ego' over the play of the urges, is naturally unfit for the task in hand here.

At this point, however, it is necessary to draw an
essential distinction in order to avert a misunder-
standing which, nowadays, threatens every statement of this kind. What we are dealing with here
is generically different from what is called self-
analysis in modern psychology. The latter, as is the
case in general with psychological analysis in our
age, is concerned to penetrate 'behind' that which
is remembered, to 'reduce' it to the real elements
assumed to have been 'repressed'. Our business is
to call to mind an occurrence as reliably, concretely
and completely remembered as possible, which is
entirely unreduced and undissected. Naturally, the
memory must be liberated from all subsequent de-
letions and trimmings, beautifications and demon-
isations; but he can do this, to whom the confrontation with himself, in the essential compass of
the past, has proved to be one of the effective forces
in the process of 'becoming what one is'. Of leading significance to him in his work of great reflection will be the unforgotten series of those moments of electric spontaneity, when the lightning
of the has-been flashed unexpectedly across the
skies of the now.

123

If the questioner seeks to apprehend the common denominator between the self-knowledge thus acquired and the analogous self-knowledge of others which has become known to him, he will gain an image of the biographically decisive beginnings of evil and good which differs notably from the usual representations and provides an important confirmation of those Old Testament tales from the dawn of man.

Insight into the second stage, to which the Ancient Iranian tales are to be related, must naturally be gained along a different path.

III. THE FIRST STAGE

HUMAN life as a specific entity, which has stepped forth from nature, begins with the experience of chaos as a condition perceived in the soul.

Only through this experience and as its materialisation could the concept of chaos, which is to be derived from no other empirical finding, arise and enter into the mythic cosmogonies.

In a period of evolution, which generally coincides with puberty without being tied to it, the human person inevitably becomes aware of the category of possibility, which of all living creatures is represented just in man, manifestly the only one for whom the real is continually fringed by the possible.

The evolving human person I am speaking of is bowled over by possibility as an infinitude. The plenitude of possibility floods over his small reality and overwhelms it. Phantasy, the imagery of possibilities which, in the Old Testament, God pronounces evil because it distracts from His divinely given reality and plays with potentialities, imposes the form of its indefiniteness upon the definiteness of the moment. The substantial threatens to be submerged in the potential. Swirling chaos, 'confusion and desolation' (Genesis 1, 2) has forced its way in.

But as, in the stage I am speaking of, everything which appears or happens to man is transformed into motor-energy, into the capacity and desire for action, so too the chaos of possibilities of being, having forced an entry, becomes a chaos of possibilities of action. It is not things which revolve in the vortex, but the possible ways of joining and overcoming them.

This impelling universal passion is not to be confounded with the so-called libido, without whose vital energy it naturally could not endure, but to reduce it to which signifies a simplification and animalisation of human reality. Urges in the psychological sense are abstractions; but we are speaking of a total concrete occurrence at a given hour of a person's life. Moreover, these urges are, *per definitionem*, 'directed toward something'; but lack of direction is characteristic of the vortex revolving within itself.

The soul driven round in the dizzy whirl cannot remain fixed within it; it strives to escape. If the ebb that leads back to familiar normality does not make its appearance, there exist for it two issues. One is repeatedly offered it: it can clutch at any object, past which the vortex happens to carry it, and cast its passion upon it; or else, in response to a prompting that is still incomprehensible to itself, it can set about the audacious work of self-unification. In the former case, it exchanges an undirected possibility for an undirected reality, in which it does what it wills not to do, what is preposterous to it, the alien, the 'evil'; in the latter, if the work meets with success, the soul has given up undirected plenitude in favour of the one taut string, the one stretched beam of direction. If the work is not successful, which is no wonder with such an unfathomable undertaking, the soul has nevertheless gained an inkling of what direction, or rather *the* direction is—for in the strict sense there is only one. To the extent to which the soul achieves unification it becomes aware of direction, becomes aware of itself as sent in quest of it. It comes into the service of good or into service for good.

Finality does not rule here. Again and again, with the surge of its enticements, universal temptation emerges and overcomes the power of the human soul; again and again innate grace arises from out of its depths and promises the utterly incredible: you can become whole and one. But always there are, not left and right, but the vortex of chaos and the spirit hovering above it. Of the two paths, one is a setting out upon no path, pseudo-decision which is indecision, flight into delusion and ultimately into mania; the other is the path, for there is only one.

The same basic structure of the occurrence, however, only become briefer and harder, we re-encounter in innumerable situations in our later lives. They are the situations in which we feel it incumbent upon us to make the decision which, from our person, and from our person as we feel it 'purposed' for us, answers the situation confronting us. Such a decision can only be taken by the whole soul that has become one; the whole soul, in whatever direction it was turned or inclined when the situation came upon us, must enter into it, otherwise we shall bring forth nothing but a stammer, a pseudo-answer, a substitute for an answer. The situations, whether more biographical or more historical in character, are always—even though often behind veils—cruelly harsh, because the unrecoverable passage of time and of our lives is so, and only with the harshness of unified decision can we prove ourselves equal to them. It is a cruelly hazardous enterprise, this becoming a whole, becoming a form, of crystallization of the soul. Everything in the nature of inclinations, of indolence, of habits, of fondness for possibilities which has been swash-buckling within us, must be overcome, and over-come, not by elimination, by suppression, for gen-uine wholeness can never be achieved like that, never a wholeness where downtrodden appetites lurk in the corners. Rather must all these mobile or static forces, seized by the soul's rapture, plunge of their own accord, as it were, into the mightiness of decision and dissolve within it. Until the soul as form has such great power over the soul as matter, until chaos is subdued and shaped into cosmos, what an immense resistance! It is thus understand-able enough that the occurrence—which at times, as we know to be the case with dreams encompass-ing a whole drama, lasts no longer than a minute —so frequently terminates in a persistent state of indecision. The anthropological retrospective view of the person (which indeed is incorrectly termed 'view', for if our memory proves strong enough we experience such past occurrences with all our senses, with the excitation of our nerves and the tension or flaccidity of our muscles) announces to us as evil all these and all other indecisions, all the moments in which we did no more than leave undone that which we knew to be good. But is evil then not, by its nature, an action? Not at all: action is only the type of evil happening which makes evil manifest. But does not evil action stem precisely from a decision to evil? The ultimate meaning of our exposition is that it too stems primarily from indecision, providing that by decision we understand, not a partial, a pseudo decision, but that of the whole soul. For a partial decision, one which leaves the forces opposing it untouched, and certainly which the soul's highest forces, being the true constructional substance of the person purposed for me, watch, pressed back and powerless, but shining in the protest of the spirit, cannot be termed decision in our sense. Evil cannot be done with the whole soul; good can only be done with the whole soul. It is done when the soul's rapture, proceeding from its highest forces, seizes upon all the forces and plunges them into the purging and transmuting fire, as into the mightiness of decision. Evil is lack of direction and that which is done in it and out of it as the grasping, seizing, devouring compelling, seducing, exploiting, humiliating, torturing and destroying of what offers itself. Good is direction and what is done in it; that which is done in it is done with the whole soul, so that in fact all the vigour and passion with which evil might have been done is included in it. In this connection is to be recalled that Talmudic interpretation of the Biblical pronouncement of God concerning imagination or the 'evil urge', whose whole vigour must be drawn into the love of God in order truly to serve Him.

The foregoing is intended and able to give no more than an anthropological definition of good and evil as, in the last instance, it is revealed to the human person's retrospection, his cognizance of himself in the course of the life he has lived. We learn to comprehend this anthropological definition as similar in nature to the biblical tales of good and evil, whose narrator must have experienced Adam as well as Kain in the abyss of his own heart. But it is neither intended nor able to provide any criterion over and above that, either for the use of theoretical meditation concerning the entities 'good' and 'evil' nor, certainly, for the use of the questioning man, who is not spared enquiry and investigation into what, in the sense of design, is good and what evil, groping and feeling his way in the obscurity of the problematics, and even doubt as to the validity of the concepts themselves. The former and the latter will have to find their criterion, or their criteria elsewhere, will have to achieve it otherwise: the meditant seeks to learn something else than what happens, the designant cannot make his choice according to whether it will lead to his soul becoming whole. Between their requirements and our anthropological insight there is only one link, which is, of course, an important one. It is the presentiment implanted in each of us, but unduly neglected in each, the presentiment of what is meant and purposed for him and for him alone—no matter whether by creation, or by 'individuation'—and to fulfil which, to become which is demanded of and entrusted to him, and the resulting possibility of comparison time and again. Here too there is a criterion, and it is an anthropological one; of course, by its nature, it can never extend beyond the sphere of the individual. It can assume as many shapes as there are individuals— and nonetheless is never relativised.

IV. THE SECOND STAGE

IT is far more difficult to ascertain the human reality corresponding to the myths of Ahriman's choice and Lucifer's downfall. It is in the nature of the matter that here the assistance of retrospection is only very rarely open to us; those who have once surrendered themselves to evil with their innermost being will hardly ever, not even after a complete conversion, be capable of that deliberate, reliably recollecting and interpreting retrospection which can alone advance our insight. In the literature of those able to recount their fate we shall almost never encounter such a report; everything confronting us in this domain is, apparently of necessity, highly coloured or sentimentalised, and so thoroughly that we are unable to distil out of it the occurrences themselves, inner and outer likewise. What psychological research on phenomena of a similar nature has brought to light are naturally purely neurotic borderline cases and, with very few exceptions, not capable of illuminating

133

our problem. Here our own observations, whose methods are adapted to that which is essential to our purpose, must set in. To supplement them, by far the richest contribution is offered by historical and, in particular, biographical literature. It is a question of concentrating our attention on those personal crises whose specific effect on the person's psychic dynamic is to render it obdurate and secretive. We then find that these crises are of two clearly distinguishable kinds: negative experiences with our environment, which denies us the confirmation of our being that we desire, underlie the one; negative experiences with oneself, in that the human person cannot say Yes to himself, underlie the other —the only one that concerns us here; we will leave aside mixed forms.

We have seen how man repeatedly experiences the dimension of evil as indecision. The occurrences in which he experiences it, however, do not remain in his self-knowledge a series of isolated moments of non-decision, of becoming possessed by the play of the phantasy with potentialities, of plunging in this possession upon that which offers itself: in self-knowledge, these moments merge into a course of indecision, as it were into a fixation in it. This negativation of self-knowledge is, of course, again and again 'repressed', as long as the will to simple self-preservation dominates that to being-able-to-affirm-oneself. To the extent, on the other hand, to which the latter asserts itself, the condition will change into one of acute auto-problematics: man calls himself in question, because his self-knowledge no longer enables him to affirm and confirm himself. This condition now either assumes a pathological form, that is, the relationship of the person to himself becomes fragile and intricate; or the person finds the way out where he hardly expected it, namely through an extreme effort of unification, which astonishes him himself in its power and effectiveness, a decisive act of decision, precisely that therefore, which in the amazingly apposite language of religion is called 'conversion'; or a third process takes place, something entitled to a special status amongst the singularities of man and to the consideration of which we must now turn.

Because man is the sole living creature known to us in whom the category of possibility is so to speak embodied, and whose reality is incessantly enveloped by possibilities, he alone amongst them all needs confirmation. Every animal is fixed in its this-being, its modifications are preordained, and when it changes into a caterpillar and into a chrys-

alis its very metamorphosis is a boundary; in everything together it remains exactly what it is, therefore it can need no confirmation; it would, indeed,
be an absurdity for someone to say to it, or for it
to say to itself: You may be what you are. Man
as man is an audacity of life, undetermined and
unfixed; he therefore requires confirmation, and he
can naturally only receive this as individual man,
in that others and he himself confirm him in his
being-this-man. Again and again the Yes must be
spoken to him, from the look of the confidant and
from the stirrings of his own heart, to liberate him
from the dread of abandonment, which is a fore-
taste of death. At a pinch, one can do without confirmation from others if one's own reaches such a
pitch that it no longer needs to be supplemented
by the confirmation of others. But not vice versa:
the encouragement of his fellow-men does not suf-
fice if self-knowledge demands inner rejection, for
self-knowledge is incontestably the more reliable.
Then man, if he cannot readjust his self-knowledge
by his own conversion, must withdraw from it the
power over the Yes and No; he must render affirmation independent of all findings and base it,
instead of on 'judgement-of-oneself', on a sovereign
willing-oneself; he must choose himself, and that

not 'as he is intended'—this image must, rather, be totally extinguished—but just as he is, as he has himself resolved to intend himself. They are recognisable, those who dominate their own self-knowledge, by the spastic pressure of the lips, the spastic tension of the muscles of the hand and the spastic tread of the foot. This attitude corresponds to what I have called the third process, which leads out of auto-problematics 'into the open': one need no longer look for being, it is here, one is what one wants and one wants what one is. It is of this that the myth is speaking when it recounts that Yima proclaimed himself his own creator. Just this too Prudentius reports of Satan, and the great legendary motif of the pact with him is clearly derived from the view that he who has achieved self-creation will be ready to assist men to it.

From this point, the meaning of that paradoxical myth of the two spirits, one of whom chose evil, not without knowing it to be evil, but as evil, is also revealed to us. The 'wicked' spirit—in whom, therefore, evil is already present, if only *in statu nascendi*—has to choose between the two affirmations: affirmation of himself and affirmation of the order, which has established and eternally establishes good and evil, the first as the affirmed and the second as the denied. If he affirms the order he must himself become 'good', and that means he must deny and overcome his present state of being. If he affirms himself he must deny and reverse the order; to the yes-position, which 'good' had occupied, he must bring the principle of his own self-affirmation, nothing else must remain worthy of affirmation than just that which is affirmed by him; his Yes to himself determines the reason and right of affirmation. If he still concedes any significance to the concept 'good', it is this: precisely that which I am. He has chosen himself, and nothing, no quality and no destiny, can any longer be signed with a No if it is his.

This too explains altogether why Yima's defection is called a lie. By glorifying and blessing himself as his own creator, he commits the lie against being, yea, he wants to raise it, the lie, to rule over being, for truth shall no longer be what he experiences as such but what he ordains as such. The narrative of Yima's life after his defection says with super-clarity all that remains to be said here.

V. EVIL AND GOOD

THE images of good and evil which have been interpreted here correspond, as I have shown, to certain anthropologically apprehensible occurrences in the life-path of the human person. They include the images of evil belonging to two different stages on this path, the Old Testament images to an earlier, the Iranian to a later; whereas the images of good refer, in the main, to the same momentum, which may occur at either the first or the second stage.

To the Biblical images of evil corresponds, in the first stage of living reality, the purpose of man to overcome the chaotic state of his soul, the state of undirected surging passion, in appearance only, instead of really overcoming it and breaking violently out of it wherever a breach can be forced, instead of achieving direction by unifying his energies—the only manner in which it can be achieved. To the ancient Persian images corresponds, in the second stage of living reality, man's endeavour to render the contradictory state, which has arisen in consequence of his lack of direction and his pseudo-decisions, bearable and even satisfying, by affirming this state, in the context of the total constitution of the personality, absolutely. In the first stage man does not choose, he merely acts; in the second he chooses himself, in the sense of his being-constituted-thus or having-become-thus. The first stage does not yet contain a 'radical evil'; whatever misdeeds are committed, their commission is not a doing of the deed but a sliding into it. In the second stage evil grows radical, because what man finds in himself is willed; whoever lends to that which, in the depths of self-awareness was time and again recognised by him as what should be negated, the mark of being affirmed, because it is his, gives it the substantial character which it did not previously possess. If we may compare the occurrence of the first stage to an eccentric whirling movement, the process of the freezing of flowing water may serve as a simile to illustrate the second.

Good, on the other hand, retains the character of direction at both stages. I have already indicated that for true human decision, that is, decision taken by the unified soul there is only One direction. This means that to whatever end the current decision is reached, in the reality of existence all the so diverse decisions are merely variations on a single one, which is continually made afresh in a single direction. This direction can be understood in two ways. Either it is understood as the direction towards the person purposed for me, which I only apprehend in such self-awareness that divides and decides, not thrusting any energy back, but transforming undirected energies into it by conferring direction upon them: I recognise ever more clearly that which is purposed for me, precisely because I confer the direction upon it and take the direction toward it—the experience of vital hours provides us with the key to this paradox, its actuality and its significance. Or else the single direction is understood as the direction toward God. This duality of comprehension, however, is no more than a duality of aspects, provided only that I do not apply the name 'God' to a projection of myself or anything of that kind, but to my creator, that is, the author of my uniqueness, which cannot be derived from within the world. My uniqueness, this unrepeatable form of being here, not analysable into any elements and not compoundable out of any, I experience as a designed or preformed one, entrusted to me for execution, although everything that affects me participates in this execution. That a unique human being is created does not mean that it is put into being for a mere existence, but for the fulfilment of a being-intention, an intention of being which is personal, not however in the sense of a free unfolding of infinite singularities, but of a realisation of the right in infinite personal shapes. For creation has a goal and the humanly right is service directed in the One direction, service of the goal of creation which we are given to surmise only to the extent necessary within this scope; the humanly right is ever the service of the single person who realises the right uniqueness purposed for him in his creation. In decision, taking the direction thus means: taking the direction toward the point of being at which, executing for my part the design which I am, I encounter the divine mystery of my created uniqueness, the mystery waiting for me.

Good conceived thus cannot be located within any system of ethical co-ordination, for all those we know came into being on its account and existed or exist by virtue of it. Every ethos has its origin in a revelation, whether or not it is still aware of and obedient to it; and every revelation is revelation of human service to the goal of creation, in which service man authenticates himself. Without authentication, that is, without setting off upon and keeping to the One direction, as far as he is able, *quantum satis*, man certainly has what he calls life, even the life of the soul, even the life of the spirit, in all freedom and fruitfulness, all standing and status—existence there is none for him without it.

7